The Road to Writing

A Step-by-Step Guide to Mark Making: 3–7

D1293040

A companion website to accompany this book is available online at:
http://education.cowley3.continuumbooks.com

Please type in the URL above to receive your unique password for access to the book's online resources.

If you experience any problems accessing the resources, please contact Continuum at: info@continuumbooks.com

Also available by Sue Cowley

Getting the Buggers into Drama, Sue Cowley
Getting the Buggers to Behave (4th edition), Sue Cowley
Getting the Buggers to Think (2nd edition), Sue Cowley
Getting the Buggers to Write (3rd edition), Sue Cowley
How to Survive your First Year in Teaching (2nd edition), Sue Cowley

The Road to Writing

A Step-by-Step Guide to Mark Making: 3–7

Sue Cowley

continuum

Continuum International Publishing Group

The Tower Building
11 York Road
London SE1 7NX

80 Maiden Lane
Suite 704
New York NY 10038

www.continuumbooks.com

British Library Cataloguing-in-Publication Data
A catalogue record for this book is available from the British Library.

ISBN: 978-1-4411-0344-4 (paperback)
        978-1-4411-0198-3 (ePub)
        978-1-4411-5164-3 (PDF)

Library of Congress Cataloging-in-Publication Data
Cowley, Sue.
  The road to writing : a step-by-step guide to mark making, 3-7 /
Sue Cowley.
    p. cm.
  Includes index.
  ISBN-13: 978-1-4411-0344-4
  ISBN-10: 1-4411-0344-9
  ISBN-13: 978-1-4411-0198-3
  ISBN-13: 978-1-4411-5164-3
  1. English language–Composition and exercises–Study and
teaching (Early childhood) I. Title.
  LB1139.5.L35C69 2012
  372.6–dc23

                                                    2012003517

Typeset by Newgen Imaging Systems Pvt Ltd, Chennai, India
Printed and bound in India

This book is dedicated to Lynne Willmott
for her commitment to our preschool,
and the children who attend it.

Contents

Acknowledgements

Many thanks to all the staff, children, parents and committee members at Stanton Drew and Pensford Preschool, both past and present. It's been a privilege and a pleasure helping to run our setting. Thanks also to all the staff, children and parents who have supported and worked with me in the 'Magazine Team' at Stanton Drew Primary School.

A huge 'thank you' goes to my photographer Manda Le Pivert for her wonderful images of the children playing, learning and making marks. My gratitude must also go to everyone at my publishers Continuum (now Bloomsbury), especially to my editor Melanie Wilson and her assistant Rosie Pattinson. A special vote of thanks as always goes to my family, who support me and who make it possible for me to write.

And finally, thanks particularly to all those children who are featured in the photographs in this book and whose writing I've used: Álvie and Edite Castellino, Jack and Niamh Bishop, Alex Bradbury, Matty Croucher and Shay O'Malley.

Introduction

A journey of a thousand miles begins with a single step.

Lao Tzu

It's amazing to think that it only takes about 6 or 7 years from the moment a baby is born, to when that same child is typically able to read and write fairly fluently. In that very short space of time, she acquires an entire spoken language (including a subconscious understanding of its grammatical rules). That same child learns how, when and why we use words to communicate. She develops the physical skills needed to support her body and to hold and manipulate a writing tool. She understands how to match spoken sounds with written letters and words, and how different kinds of texts work. And she is confident and motivated to put her own words down on the page. When you stop to think about it, it's an incredible achievement.

Learning to write, and to write well, is crucial in a child's chance of educational success. Writing is there, right at the heart of pretty much every subject taught within schools. It's something that children must do, each and every day. And if they *can't* do it, if they *can't* access and use language, it's very likely that they will become disaffected and start to misbehave. During my teaching career I've taught children from the age of two, right through to the age of 18. I've seen young children who already have a secure grasp of the written word, but equally I've come across secondary age students who simply cannot, or will not, write. Something went wrong for these children during their early years. For some reason, they stumbled off the road to writing, and no one was able to get them back on track. Whether you're a nursery or reception teacher, an early years professional, a nursery nurse, a preschool leader or assistant, a teaching assistant or a child minder, this book is for you. Because whatever your role is, as an early years educator you are hugely important in setting your children off on the right course.

This book is designed to guide you and your children, step by step, along the road to writing. From the very early marks to the thrill of those first proper words and sentences, I give you all the key information you need about the process of learning to write. You will learn about the skills, attributes, attitudes, concepts and abilities that you must help your children develop or grasp. I will encourage you to have confidence in the approaches that you use, showing you how to boost your children's motivation to make marks, and helping you inspire *all* your children to become lifelong writers. Although theory has its value, this book is very much rooted in the practicalities of working with young children. As with all my books, it is written in a user-friendly and accessible way, with no jargon or difficult terminology.

The road to writing is a tough one, scattered with many potential obstacles. Each child is a unique individual, and the journey along the road will be different for each one. Some children will skip quickly along the road, hardly stumbling, picking up the skills required without any trouble at all. For these children, success breeds success, confidence feeds on confidence. Other children will struggle with the journey, finding it hard to acquire the skills or the motivation to succeed, perhaps because of a specific learning or behavioural issue, or a difficult home background. Some children will struggle particularly with one area, while others will struggle to make any progress at all. In this book you will find ideas to help *all* your children make the journey down the road to writing.

The road to writing can, should, indeed *must* be a joyous and exciting journey – writing is not a dull, dry craft, but a vibrant, exciting act of communication. This book shows you how to take your children on the most interactive, multisensory, adventurous, inspirational and dramatic route possible. Yes, there are risks along the way, and things may get messy, but that's the nature of working in the early years. Yes, skills and self-discipline are crucial, but without engagement and motivation, they are of very little value. In this book you'll find loads of practical activities which will help your young mark makers develop into confident, fluent writers, able to express themselves through the written word. Wherever you see an icon like this 🖐, you'll also find detailed information about some 'Practical Projects' that you can try out in your setting. Wherever you work, the ideas in this book are ones you can use, straight away – today!

Our journey begins with a bit of preparation; before we head out we must have a think about what our map looks like, who gets to lead the way and also what equipment we need to take with us. Once we set off, each section of this book focuses on one 'signpost' that your children will meet on their journey to becoming writers. Your children might not pass these stages or signposts in the exact same order as you find them here (it can be a bendy road). Some children will reach several signposts almost simultaneously; others will struggle with particular aspects of the route. Whatever your children need to become writers, you should find the tools here to help them keep travelling forward.

Please note that this book is not about getting children to 'meet targets' or 'achieve levels' – you don't fatten the pig by weighing it. Nor is it about how to please inspectors, government officials or local authority advisers. It certainly isn't a highly structured set of guidelines for teaching writing, which come with a trade mark, a clever sounding title or a hefty price tag. Rather, this book is simply a repository of good ideas, good practice and inspirational activities drawn from my own experience and from a wide range of professional sources. It's a road map which draws on all the great things that early years teachers and practitioners do every day in their preschool, nursery and school settings.

If I have one hope for how this book can work for you, it is that it helps you trust in your professional judgement, in your gut instinct about what works: that you are encouraged to believe that *you* know what is right for *your* children. Because if you always sway with the latest fads and fashions in teaching, you will drive yourself and your children to distraction. On the other hand, in education, if you stand still long enough, eventually someone will say that what you have always done was right all along! Good practice, self belief and a balanced approach is always going to be the best route to take.

Things move very quickly in education, and on the internet as well. You can find up-to-date materials and links in the companion website, for instance details of how the ideas in this book link up with the latest government guidance on teaching in the early years. At the time of writing, the Early Years Foundation Stage (EYFS) was under review, with promises of a slimmed-down version due September 2012. In the companion website, you'll find also case studies which show you how different children might take different routes down the road to writing. And you'll find downloadable checklists, to use when auditing the current provision in your setting. Look for the mouse symbol 🖱 throughout this book, to find out what other useful materials are in the companion site.

I'll finish by wishing you and your children all the best of luck on your journey along the road to writing. As educators, we are hugely fortunate to be able to help our children achieve the gift of becoming writers. It's a gift which allows them to express themselves, their ideas, their opinions, their creativity, through the medium of language. It's a gift that my own teachers gave to me, many years ago, and which allows me to communicate with you right now. And to have the chance to make such a difference in a child's life is, to my mind, nothing short of a miracle. Go forth, and perform magic!

Sue Cowley
www.suecowley.co.uk
www.celebrate-writing.co.uk

Please note: I have used a random mix of 'she' and 'he' throughout this book when referring to children and practitioners.

Starting Points: A Map for the Journey

In this section …

- Create a 'map' of effective practice for the journey
- Consider who leads the learning, when they lead it and why
- Examine the vital role played by resources
- Find ideas for getting creative with resourcing
- Help your children access resources in your setting
- Use checklists to help you audit where you are right now

Consider this …

Our journey along the *Road to Writing* has a clear destination – for each child to become a confident and able writer, keen to communicate their ideas and with a love of the written word. It's not an easy task, but that's what this book will help you to achieve. Before we set out on our journey, it's important to think about how the map will be drawn, who gets to hold it and what route we are going to take. Or, in other words, to consider where we stand on some key questions:

- Who leads the learning?
- What is the learning going to look like?
- What's the best way to make the learning happen?
- What resources do we need to achieve the learning?

Who leads the learning?

Perhaps you see yourself more in the classic teacher role, getting your children to learn to write by using plenty of whole class teaching techniques and adult-directed tasks? Or maybe you prefer to take on the role of a facilitator, being there to support the child's learning, in whatever direction he or she chooses to take it? In reality, of course, you'll be a bit of both, depending partly on the age group with whom you work. Sometimes you'll want to direct or intervene, at other times you'll wish to stand back and observe. Using the metaphor of a journey, on which this book is based, you'll need to think about how far you are going to:

- Let the child wander off on his own, asking him to draw his own map along the way, figuring out what route he wants to take;
- Give the child a rough guide as to some interesting places she might visit on her journey, offering a map that she can use when she needs or wants;
- Follow behind the child, but intervene if he gets lost, or if he needs to take a different route;
- Put up signposts so that the journey is clear, and the best or quickest route is taken;
- Teach the child the skills she needs to reach her destination, and get her to practice them en route;
- Guide the child through the entire journey to make sure he reaches his destination in the fastest possible time.

The decisions about who leads the learning will be based on:

- ✓ The age group you teach;
- ✓ The ability levels of the children;
- ✓ Your knowledge of each individual child – how much support he needs, how fast she can progress down the road, how ready he is to learn these skills;
- ✓ How quickly you feel your children need to pick up these skills, that is how much importance you place on writing happening quickly, as opposed to the value of other types of learning;
- ✓ The behaviour of the group – sometimes 'engaging the class' needs to take priority over 'progressing their skills';
- ✓ Your own personal philosophy of education, and of early years teaching;

✓ The kind of space you have to work in, and the resources you
have available;

✓ The timing of your sessions, or of your school day.

You may come under pressure to base your decisions on other factors
as well. As far as is possible and sensible, resist these pressures and trust
in your own professional judgement. If you truly know and understand
these children, then believe that *you* know best what they need. Factors
on which to place less emphasis include:

× What your head teacher would think;

× What OFSTED (the Office for Standards in Education) would say;

× Pressure from parents and carers to work in a particular way;

× What the current version of the early years curriculum
demands.

As I said in the introduction, try your very hardest not to be swayed
by the latest fads and fashions or the current educational 'buzz words'.
Just to give you a quick example, anyone coming into teaching right
now might think that the idea of a three part lesson is some brand new
innovation. But when I first started out in teaching, many years ago,
believe it or not our lessons did already have a beginning, a middle and
an end.

Thinking about child-initiated learning

In recent years, the emphasis within early years education has been very
much on the children initiating their own learning. We have certainly
moved far away from the situation where adults working in nurseries
and playgroups got children to churn out 20 copies of the same picture,
using the same resources, stuck in exactly the same place. (An activity
which was often done to please the parents rather than to help the child
learn and develop.) These days, teachers and practitioners are confident
about allowing young children to make choices about where they play
and what they play with, and to follow the children's interests in the way
that they plan. The process of a child discovering what she enjoys, and

learning through her play, is a key feature of modern early years settings. After all, before a child reaches formal school starting age this is not a statutory part of their education. It is a time for children to develop at their own pace and enjoy their play.

However, as with all things in life, balance is essential. Child-initiated learning does not mean that the adult never intervenes, or never guides what the child does. Nor does it mean that we never introduce the child to new ideas, experiences, activities or themes. As adults, we've been along this road before and we know what the pitfalls and dangers are and how to get over the obstacles. Why on earth would we *not* help children progress more quickly and easily by sometimes making a gentle intervention?

It's really important for us as educators to make decisions based on what we know about our children, in our particular setting. We can develop activities around their interests, but equally we have a professional duty to introduce them to a variety of experiences. This is particularly so for those children who haven't been to a beach, or dug in the mud to plant a seed, or walked along a balance beam or seen dinosaur skeletons in a museum. A child's interests will be limited by his immediate experience of the world – our job is to widen and enrich that experience where we can. Similarly, some children will be ready for more adult guidance or direction much earlier on, to move them forward with their learning; other children will need to wait until they are much older before being ready for adult-directed tasks. The key is being responsive to the individual child.

A spectrum of teaching and learning

There are essentially three main types of learning within an early years setting or classroom. Most activities that a child does will fall somewhere on a spectrum between being totally child-initiated, to being completely adult led:

Child's Choice	Adult's Input	Adult's Choice
Child-initiated learning	*Adult-initiated learning*	*Adult-directed learning*
The child chooses where he wants to play, and what he wants to play with	The adult creates an activity or challenge to 'initiate' a response from the children	The adult sets up a task, and asks or insists that the children complete it

Of course, if you stop to consider it fully, even in the most child-initiated situation possible adults are still making decisions about the learning. For a start, we decide what resources to offer the children, and where to put these resources. Even if we claim that the children are given a 'free choice' of what to play with, the choice is only between those resources that we actually have within the setting. We may also decide how and when to intervene with the play that's happening, or when to introduce a 'next step' for an individual child, based on their self-initiated learning.

Interestingly, this spectrum of learning is mirrored much higher up the school. Even at secondary level, teachers are now questioning how far students should control and initiate their own learning, and how much input and direction the teacher should give. The important question to pose is: *how will they learn this best?* The old fashioned model of the teacher being in charge, and always saying what happens, is being challenged throughout the sector. At the same time, though, there are certain skills, facts and approaches which are best learned by direct teaching from an adult. Equally, there are particular disciplines and skills (letter formation and handwriting being prime examples) where adult-directed practice is by far the most efficient way to learn.

Finding a balance

2–3 years: For the younger children, it's appropriate and sensible to use mainly child-initiated learning – to respond to and build on the child's interests. The adult might initiate some activities which would benefit the child, or offer fresh experiences, but there is no insistence that these must be accessed or completed. Children of this age do not normally have the focus to stick at a particular task for any great length of time. And why would they? There is so much about the world that they want to discover!

3–4 years: For preschool-aged children and those who will move into a Reception class in the following academic year, a mixture of mostly child-initiated, some adult-initiated and some adult-directed learning is appropriate. The more able or advanced children within this group will be able to focus well on adult-initiated or adult-directed activities for part of the time they are with you.

4–5 years: Once the children reach the top end of this age group, and move into the statutory part of their schooling, they are typically ready to learn with more adult direction. For Reception children aged 4–5 years, adult-directed or guided learning becomes an important feature of the school day, alongside time to play and initiate their own learning. There are some key skills that the children need to be taught, rather than us expecting them to pick up everything by osmosis. Children won't 'initiate' correct letter formation by accidentally stumbling across the skills required. They are going to have to practice and persevere.

5–6 years and beyond: As children move into the first key stage, they typically encounter a more formal style of learning. Certainly, there will be more whole class teaching with this age group, and the children should be able to focus for longer periods of time. You will also want to get them practising specific writing skills, such as handwriting, on a regular basis. These can be done as a short activity by the whole class or by individuals and small groups of children who are ready. There will also be plenty of chances for the children to have input into the direction their learning takes, and to take ownership of the activities that they do.

Guiding the children's learning

Child-initiated learning does not mean that the adult simply stands back and does nothing, or only joins in with the child when asked. You still have a key role to play within this type of learning, because you can guide what the children are learning based on your knowledge and understanding of individuals. The quality of the child's experience will be greatly enhanced by:

- ✓ The way that you set up activities and areas and whether they inspire the child to want to try them;
- ✓ How effective you are at observing the child and working out what he might need or want to learn about next;
- ✓ How well you can plan experiences that allow or encourage her to learn these 'next steps';
- ✓ How clever you are at incorporating and extending a child's interests in the activities you offer;
- ✓ The kind of resources you are able to offer, and how creatively you use these resources;
- ✓ How easily the children can access the resources.

Resources for mark making

The next key question to consider before setting out on our journey is what kind of things we are going to take with us. What sort of items will make our journey safe, fun and interesting? What might we need to use along the way? What about the people who are travelling with us? What do they need to be like?

The quality of the activities you offer your children depends a great deal on the resources you offer to back them up. That is not to say that you have to spend a fortune on buying brand new pens and paints, or fancy paper or the latest toys. With some imagination, and a bit of lateral thinking, many resources can be created for little or nothing. See the following sections for plenty of inspiration.

Effective resources

Because resources play such a key part in the learning that your children do each day, it's important to think carefully about what makes a 'good' resource. The best resources:

- ✓ Have a variety of purposes and possibilities – you and your children can use them in a whole range of different ways;
- ✓ Offer multisensory elements or features, so that they appeal to as many of the child's senses as possible;
- ✓ Are sturdy, high quality, well made and will last you and your setting for a long time – this is especially important for pack away settings;
- ✓ Really appeal to the children, perhaps because they are interesting to touch, brightly coloured, larger than life and so on;
- ✓ Are appropriate for the children size wise, for instance chairs and desks that allow them to sit in the correct position to write.

The magic of multisensory resources

Much of the time in educational settings, children use only a limited range of senses, and often in a rather limited way (particularly once they start at school). Day-to-day, the two main senses being used will be sight and hearing: they look at the teacher, board or book, they listen to the teacher and talk with each other. Touch makes an appearance too, because of course they have to hold a pencil to write or to do their sums. But smell and taste often take a back seat, or get forgotten completely.

In order to get the best and most inspirational use out of resources, and to encourage writing skills in the most effective way, you need to offer plenty of multisensory experiences to your children. You might:

- ✓ Light a scented candle to create a relaxing atmosphere for learning;
- ✓ Play some music quietly in the background while the children write;
- ✓ Offer the children a 'feely bag', full of loads of different textures;
- ✓ Use photos, film or paintings to inspire a response, perhaps based around genre;
- ✓ Blindfold volunteers, to smell or taste some foods;
- ✓ Write 'letters in the air' using torches (or light sabres!) in a darkened room or a black out tent.

You'll find loads of suggestions for multisensory activities and resources, throughout this book.

Plastic toys/resources

Plastic toys tend to dominate many children's homes, and are a feature of most early years settings. Generally speaking, there is quite a bit of negativity towards plastic toys within the early years sector. Plastic toys do have advantages, in that they are:

- ✓ Easy to clean;
- ✓ Long lasting;
- ✓ Safe;
- ✓ Typically cheap to buy;
- ✓ Can be very lifelike, for example plastic foods;
- ✓ Can help you offer a range of cultural images, for example lifelike babies from different racial backgrounds;
- ✓ Are often very popular with the children (a set of pink plastic ponies are a big hit at our preschool and the staff refuse point blank to get rid of them).

On the downside, plastic toys and resources:

- ✕ Have a limited sensory appeal for the children;
- ✕ Are not particularly environmentally friendly;

    × Often use bright 'unreal' colours;
    × Tend to have a limited range of uses;
    × Can sometimes be rather stereotyped (e.g. pink plastic ponies).

However, that is not to say that plastic toys and resources do not have a valuable role to play within your setting, nor that we should be sniffy about using them. Consider the humble Lego brick, which was voted 'Toy of the Century' just before the turn of the millennium. Lego is a fantastic resource which can help your children develop a whole myriad of skills – building, construction, creativity, role play and so on and on.

Natural toys/resources

Wooden toys, and resources made of natural rather than man-made materials, are instinctively appealing to early years educators. We want our children to connect with the natural world, and to have access to a range of sensory experiences, particularly around touch. Toys and resources made of natural materials have a range of advantages and benefits. Typically they:

    ✓ Have a far wider sensory appeal for the children;
    ✓ Are an environmentally friendly alternative (so long as they are made from sustainable sources);
    ✓ Tend to use softer, pastel colours;
    ✓ Sometimes offer a wider range of uses than their plastic counterparts;
    ✓ Are often made with a specific multicultural learning purpose in mind, for instance cotton role play clothes from countries around the world.

However, on the downside, they:

    × Can be harder to keep clean or to sanitize than their plastic counterparts;
    × Are surprisingly sometimes not so long lasting either (we've had trouble with the longevity of wooden balance bikes and wooden screens);
    × Are often much more expensive to buy;
    × Can require more maintenance, for example a wooden climbing frame may need annual checks and repairs;

× Can lack some of the lifelike qualities of plastic alternatives, for example wooden foods tend to be very toy like;

× Sometimes come with 'politically correct' credentials that make them seem appealing to adults without us questioning their true value for play;

× Are not necessarily as popular with the children, who tend not to have the same warm attachment adults might have to 'real' (i.e. wooden) toys.

Real objects

Some early years approaches, such as Montessori, advocate the use of real objects wherever possible. Rather than children learning to use toy versions of every day objects, the idea is that they get used to handling and using the real thing as part of their learning and development. This would mean using real versions of plates, cups, locks, keys, foods, and so on.

The benefits of using real objects include:

✓ The learning is real and true to life;

✓ There are many chances for multisensory exploration;

✓ Children become more confident and independent about handling and using these objects in their day-to-day lives;

✓ Many of these real life objects are great for developing fine motor skills and dexterity, for instance using knives for cutting or proper gardening tools;

✓ Children learn to manage 'real life' risk and to understand how to use objects with care;

✓ Seeing real life objects in an educational situation tends to really engage and interest the children.

Equally, as with all types of resources, there are some downsides or potential issues to consider:

× There may be risks involved in handling real objects, for instance in using china cups or plates, where there is a risk of breakage;

× Storage can be an issue, particularly with fragile or perishable items;

× Parents and carers may feel nervous about their children using real objects.

To minimize any risks, when using real objects it is wise to:

✓ Use them in small groups, or with individuals;

✓ Ensure that there is close adult supervision;

✓ Opt for 'child size' versions of adult tools (for instance at our preschool we use 'Gardener's Apprentice' tools in our garden/ on our allotment – these are high quality versions of adult tools, simply made in a child's size);

✓ Take an overview of any other activities that are going on while you have real objects on offer – aim to pre-empt any potential issues, for instance a particularly lively activity right next to your priceless tea set;

✓ Reassure any worried parents about your risk assessment proce-dures and how staff supervize the children;

✓ Think about any children in your setting who have Special Educational Needs (SEN) – is it appropriate and safe for them to use these real objects?

'Real' or handmade resources

As well as real objects, make the most of any 'real resources' that you can get hold of – often recycled, organic or natural materials that you happen to have to hand, ones that you find in the great outdoors, or ones that you hand make yourself. These resources are typically great for their multi-purpose nature – you can build dens with them, screen off a reading area, make a space rocket, turn them into seats or use them for art – the only limit really is your and your children's imagination! These materials are usually either free to get hold of, or very cheap indeed. They include:

✓ Large pieces of material – choose a whole range of types for maximum adaptability, including:

  – See through materials, such as net and gauze (try charity shops for cheap net curtains),

  – Camouflage style materials, including nets,

  – Large bed sheets for den building,

  – Materials from different cultural backgrounds, for instance sari fabric or material with an African print;

✓ Cardboard boxes – ask parents to bring in any spares, or visit a packaging or storage company for those giant wardrobe sized boxes;

✓ Large flat sheets of cardboard (for instance those used for pack-aging A1 flipcharts);

✓ Spare building or garden landscaping materials – rocks, bricks, pebbles, sections of drainpipe;
✓ Natural 'found' materials, ones that you have grown yourself or sourced from others (e.g. approach a local tree surgeon for some logs):
  – Pine cones, pumpkin seeds,
  – Leaves, conkers, sticks,
  – Tree trunks and sections of log (great for seats and stepping stones).

Take your children for a walk to gather found materials, or ask parents to collect these with their children, to bring in. Ask local companies (DIY stores, builders' merchants, offices) whether you can take any spare materials off their hands. In the West Country, an organization called 'Scrapstore' offers a huge range of cheap recycled materials for early years settings. See the companion website for more details.

When you're considering a new resource for your setting or classroom, don't automatically turn to the latest catalogue of resources. It's my experience as a teacher that the children love resources that you make for them yourself. It says something special when you put your own time and effort into making a resource for the class. In the past, I've made a 'noise-o-meter' and a 'weather rewards chart' among others. In the photo below, you can see Alex posting his letter in a very handmade looking postbox!

Displaying 'real' resources

Children are typically fascinated by the objects, items and creatures that they find outside. A strange shaped stone becomes a 'dinosaur's tooth', a piece of quartz becomes a priceless 'crystal', a squished hedgehog is studied as you pass it each day. A lovely idea is to make or buy a 'Cabinet of Curiosities' – a cabinet where the children can display their found objects.

Organizing and accessing resources

Resources are most useful, and most likely to be used, if they can be accessed easily by both staff and children, and preferably sometimes by parents as well. The way that you organize your resources will depend a great deal on the kind of setting you're in, the kind of storage spaces you have available and the age group with which you work. Whatever your situation, there are certain key features of a well organized set of resources:

- ✓ Keep them tidy, by having a regular time to sort through and reorganize;
- ✓ Label them, using both visual and printed labels;
- ✓ If a resource has not been used for 6–12 months or more, either use it tomorrow or give it away;
- ✓ Never keep things 'just in case' they might come in handy at some undefined point in the future;
- ✓ Edit your resources regularly – often they build up over time as you add more new items;
- ✓ Be ruthless with yourself – once a year, get all your resources out and work your way through them. Prioritize what you keep according to how useful it is, and also how often it is used. Stop when your cupboards are full, then steel yourself to get rid of all the rest;
- ✓ Less is more when it comes to resources – that way things get used in a more creative way, and they are more likely to be treated carefully. Aim for uncluttered methods of storage and organization, rather than ramming every last item into your cupboards;
- ✓ Find ways to make the resources as accessible as possible to your children, so that they can make genuine choices about

what they'd like to play with. (See the sections below for advice on making this happen.);

✓ Keep an up to date inventory – often there will be fantastic resources that you didn't know were there, or had forgotten about or that you know are there somewhere, but simply cannot find.

Day-to-day storage

The vast majority of early years settings and primary schools will give each child a way to store his or her day-to-day items. A unit with a set of named plastic trays, one per child, is usually the best solution. Book bags, learning journeys, pictures, WOW slips, newsletters and so on can all be stored in the child's tray. The child's name is clearly labelled on the front of the tray, preferably with a picture alongside it that is familiar to the child. The same picture could be used on his peg, and on a registration board as well. Children, parents and staff can then use these trays to communicate with each other.

Resources and pack away settings

If you're in a pack away early years setting, where you have to put all your resources away at the end of each session, you will have to think creatively about how you store and access resources. You will have to be really ruthless about the quantity, type and usefulness of those resources you put into storage each day. In these situations, it can be hard for you to offer the children free choice of resources. There are a number of ways in which you can increase choice for the children:

✓ Have a 'choices' board, with a selection of laminated pictures which show the resources available, so that the children can choose from these;

✓ Have a 'choices' book, so that the children can flick through to see what you have, and make requests based on their interests;

✓ Have clear boxes in your cupboards, clearly labelled with a picture on the front, so that you can take the children in to choose their own resources;

✓ Use 'wheel out' units with clear trays in them, again labelled with pictures of what is inside.

When you're setting up your room, it's a great idea to leave a space labelled 'Children's Choice'. Consult with the children in the morning, to find out what they would like set out in that space that day.

The space as a resource

The space you have, and the way that you lay it out, will have a powerful impact on the children's experience within that space. A key part of learning to write is feeling inspired to make marks and being able to focus and concentrate effectively. Your children will learn best (and you will teach best) if your space:

✓ Feels bright and open;
✓ Is uncluttered;
✓ Is easy to move around (both for teacher/practitioner and for children);
✓ Has clearly divided areas for different learning or for different activities (you could use physical dividers, for example screens, but equally it can work to have a different kind of flooring);
✓ Has a communal space (usually a rug) where the whole group can meet;
✓ Encourages reasonable levels of noise, rather than excessive volume;
✓ Offers quiet areas, as well as busy ones;
✓ Provides areas for quiet reflection, for instance a comfy sofa where children can sit together to chat.

Use the 'Space as a Resource' checklist, and the 'Space Audit' at the end of the book to think more about how you use your space, and how it encourages or discourages mark making and writing (see p. 179).

Parents and carers in the space

Consider how you will use the space during the drop off and registration part of your day. Think about the role that parents can play in helping their children to settle quickly and to feel happy and confident. Consider too how parents can be encouraged to support their child's learning and development, and particularly their communication, language and literacy skills. For instance getting involved by helping their child choose a new reading book.

The way that you involve parents and carers within the space will depend on the age group you're working with, but also on the kind of space you have, and any whole school considerations (for instance if parents are asked to drop their children at the gate). Consider whether you want to welcome parents into the space, and ask them to help the child complete parts of the routine, or whether you would prefer the children to be as independent as possible.

Displays within the space

Displays are a great way of making your space feel inviting and welcoming. They can also be very beneficial in helping your children build up their communication and literacy skills. By seeing print around the place, particularly where it is specific and relevant, your children learn naturally that print conveys meaning. For instance a 'girl' symbol and the word 'Girls' on the toilets, or a 'Welcome' poster in a variety of different community languages.

Displays also offer a great way of celebrating your children's writing – of publishing the learning for all to see. Seeing *their* writing on the wall of *their* classroom, nursery or preschool is a really motivating factor for children of any age. Your writing displays might include:

- ✓ Alphabet displays – the larger the better (one display per letter if possible);
- ✓ Displays of the phonemes you've been working on with the class;
- ✓ Word level displays;
- ✓ Word 'bank' displays, for instance a 'Phonics Tree' or a set of vocabulary/openers for older or more fluent writers;
- ✓ Displays to support the children's writing (how to form letters, how to join handwriting);
- ✓ Displays to support the staff (e.g. questions to ask, cues for observations, how and when to make an SEN referral);
- ✓ Examples of the children's mark making/writing.

Top tips for displays

Get creative with the way that you present displays, and where you put them. Don't use them as wallpaper – make sure that you change them regularly. Remember that displaying children's work can act as a powerful motivator – you are, effectively, publishing it. Here are some of my top tips for displays:

- ✓ Hang net curtain wire along the walls, and peg displays onto this;
- ✓ Use room dividers for a dual purpose, adding displays to each side;
- ✓ Hang lines across your room, to peg up words, ideas or pictures;
- ✓ Use mini wooden craft pegs to peg up writing on a smaller scale (for instance a line of string on which the children peg up a series of images from a story in the correct order);
- ✓ Use Velcro to create 'word bank' displays;
- ✓ Display words and images in unusual places – on the ceiling, under a table, on the side of a shed;
- ✓ Graphic displays can work well in catching the eye (e.g. a pure black and white or black and silver display looks very striking);
- ✓ Windows can offer a great surface for displaying writing, particularly where you can make use of the light shining through your displays (for instance with 'stained glass' cellophane).

Key questions about displays

Displaying the children's work takes time and effort, so it's definitely worth thinking about how you do it and, indeed, why. It's tempting to throw some children's work up on the walls, just to 'get it done'. It's equally tempting to bung up some posters or images that tick the equality and diversity boxes, just so that you can say that you've covered that aspect of learning. But it's important to think realistically about whether your displays enhance the mark making and writing activities that are done in your setting, rather than simply seeing them as a kind of wallpaper to brighten things up.

Use the following steps to ensure that your displays really make an impact on the learning that takes place within your setting:

Choose a time when there are no children in the setting

Step outside the room, pause and breathe deeply

Take a few moments to empty your mind of any preconceptions

Walk into the space, looking at it completely afresh

Aim to see it as though you are a child, viewing it for the first time

What do you notice? Is anything missing?

Use the Displays Audit (see p. 180) to examine and reflect on your displays

The 'working wall'

A 'working wall' display is one that you and your children create together. It's a display which is a 'work in progress', as opposed to a 'finished product'. As you follow a particular theme, topic or area of learning you gradually add to the working wall, referring back to it as you go. A working wall is a bit like those whiteboards that you see in a detective drama – as the evidence, facts and characters in the case are discovered, the whiteboard gets covered in writing. The working wall mirrors the way that our minds work, helping the children understand how they can make connections between ideas, and within their writing.

For instance your working wall might be:

✓ Based around a 'letter of the week' – the children add words starting with this letter, bring in objects that begin with this sound, paint pictures that link to the sound. You can add those 'talking buttons' where the children record a short extract of text or sound.

✓ Created around a brainstorm, or a mind map on a class topic ('The Great Fire of London') – as you study the topic, the children add in images of key characters, key vocabulary, historical details.

✓ Based on a story – for example 'The Gruffalo', where the children build up their impression of the key characters (adding tusks and warts to the Gruffalo), pin up the sequence of events in the story, write out key phrases.

✓ Designed to gather facts or information over the course of studying a specific area. For instance when looking at growth in Science, you could start with a large picture of a plant, then work to label this, add colour, facts about how plants grow and so on.

People as a resource

It's the real life, person-to-person, human aspects of being a teacher that I really love – working with other teachers, with support staff, with the children, with parents. For all the wonderful strides made by technology in recent years, this is the one aspect of education that really cannot be replicated on a computer screen.

Staff as a resource

Within an early years setting such as a preschool or a nursery, there may be a fairly large number of staff working alongside each other, or in a series of different rooms. Once into the mainstream school environment, there are likely to be less adults in the room (a teacher and perhaps one or two support staff). However many staff you have with you, they play a key part in supporting your children in developing their writing.

To get the very best out of your staff:

✓ Encourage your staff to see themselves as a team – talk about 'us' and 'we' rather than 'I' and 'you';

✓ Plan together, as a team, in the best interests of the children;

✓ Look for the best in others, supporting and encouraging those who need development, rather than turning to criticism and negativity;

✓ See continued training and development as a key aim for your team;

✓ Capitalize on their interests – for instance if a staff member is particularly interested in Makaton, encourage her to pursue that interest;

✓ Share the knowledge around – where a member of staff is particularly skilled or knowledgeable in one area, get him to disseminate that information to the team;

✓ Delegate responsibility, to allow people to feel a sense of ownership over their day-to-day work.

Getting parents involved

The more closely you can involve parents in their children's learning, the better the chances are that your children will move swiftly and easily along the road to writing. Ironically, it's pretty much always the case in education that it's easy enough to reach those parents who do all the 'right things' for their children at home, but it's much harder to reach those parents who most need your help and support.

I've found that the key to working well with parents is to make them feel welcome, and to keep doing it, over and over again. Throw down the invitations to get involved one after another, but try not to get cynical or disaffected if they don't take you up on your offer. Take great care not to come across as patronizing, nor to tell others your views on how they should bring up their children, or what exactly they are getting wrong. Instead, take the same approaches that you know work with young children: persistence, belief, praise, positivity, creativity and then a bit more persistence!

The approaches that I've found work best for getting parents involved include to:

✓ Invite them in to see a presentation by staff, or children, and/or to take part in a workshop;

✓ Use lots of different forms to communicate, and do it frequently and informally;

✓ Send home regular newsletters, with lots of information, rather than just a list of complaints;

✓ Set up a website and preferably a blog as well, so that they can find out what the children are doing day-to-day in the setting;

✓ Use both texts and emails as a form of instant communication.

And finally . . .

With your map in place, your team primed and your rucksack packed, it's time to set off with your children on the wonderful journey of discovery that is the road to writing.

I Know How to Communicate 1

In this section . . .

- Learn more about verbal and non-verbal communication
- 'Read' what your children say – even whey they are not talking!
- Enhance the role of talk within your setting
- Encourage your children to listen more effectively
- Understand how to use high quality talk

Consider this . . .

The urge to communicate our needs, thoughts, ideas, wishes or opinions is there right from the moment we are born. You can hear it in the cries of a tired, hungry or teething baby, or the whinges or tantrums of a toddler. Even before we develop the ability to form words, we can still let other people know what we want or feel, through gestures, expressions and noises.

Right from the word 'go', babies and young children are building a network of connections between their brain cells (neurons). The more that their parents and other people talk with and stimulate a young child, the more of these connections will be formed. A child who experiences a rich environment, full of varied sensory experiences and lots of high quality talk, will inevitably become a better and more confident communicator. Even if a child has not had access to this rich, varied and talk filled environment *before* they arrive at your setting, your input still has the potential to make a huge difference.

Face, hands, body – non-verbal communication

Imagine for a moment that you are a baby again. Your world is a strange, confusing place full of big creatures who make noises that you don't understand. There are a few familiar faces – mummy, daddy, big brother, grandma – and you very quickly get used to and respond to these faces. You quickly learn that a smile means someone loves you, and you can pick out the sound and smell of your mum. When you feel hungry, you need to get this information across to these big creatures, so that they feed you. So, you use sound (waaahhh!), combined with a facial expression (making a sucking movement with your lips) to get that message across. From the very start we use communication to make sense of our world, and to get what we need or want.

Before they acquire language, babies make use of facial expression, gestures, signs and sounds to try and get us to understand. A 1-year-old might wave 'goodbye' to grandma, or point at a toy that she can't reach. And even before they understand the individual words, young children are constantly 'reading' what we say, through how we look as well as how we sound. One of the key skills of the early years practitioner or teacher is the ability to communicate in both verbal and non-verbal ways. All the time you are showing your children that spoken language (and its counterpart, non-verbal communication) is a great way to get your message across.

To encourage and inspire your young communicators, make sure that you:

- Use a bright, open face and a genuine smile, to show you like your children;
- Exaggerate your use of tone – sound *very* happy, *very* interested – young children are still learning to read expressions so will benefit from this emphasis;
- Really *listen* to what your children want to tell you: don't impose your ideas on them, be open to what they say and respond naturally;
- Become sensitive to non-verbal clues that tell you about a child's emotions or needs;
- Adapt your own approaches as you read these clues and cues.

A key skill for the early years practitioner is learning how to join in with a game or activity that the children are doing, without putting them off or causing them to 'freeze up'. The Do's and Don'ts below will help you to get it right:

Do

✓ Observe for a moment before moving into the play, to get a feel for what is going on. Listen closely to what the children are saying to each other.

✓ Use a question to introduce yourself into the play – *'Do you mind if I join in?'* or *'Wow, that looks exciting, can I have a go too?'*

✓ Use a bright, interested tone and open facial expressions.

✓ Immediately come down to their level, crouching beside the children rather than standing over them.

✓ Let the children give you orders and instructions.

✓ Play around with language while you're involved with the play – for instance singing a song that relates to the play, or playing around with letter sounds – *'Tommy's tower is tall and terribly tremendous!'*

✓ Sometimes, start the play yourself, and wait for the children to join you. (This is a useful technique for encouraging the children to access an area they wouldn't immediately choose for themselves.)

Don't

✗ Impose your own ideas, instructions or rules on the children's play – *'You should do it like this . . .'.*

✗ Jump in with a closed question, designed to test for a right/ wrong answer – *'How many blocks are in your tower, Johnny?'* This tends to have the effect of closing down the play.

✗ Step suddenly out of the play to note down an observation for the child's learning journey/profile. Respect the play enough to only come out of it when it's appropriate.

See 'Practitioner Talk' further on in this section, for lots more about effective communication.

How talk develops

When a baby cries, she is trying to communicate what she wants. At first it is often very hard for new parents to tell what their baby wants – is it food, sleep, attention, a fresh nappy? As the baby and parents get to know each other it becomes easier for the parents to distinguish one cry from another, with non-verbal clues and cues providing a helpful back up. It takes a while for babies to progress from babbling to their first real words, and for most parents that first year is a bit of a guessing game in which they try and anticipate what the crying baby requires.

There is a balance to be achieved between trying to meet a growing baby's needs, but at the same time not encouraging them to be over dependent and to feel that they need only squeak and the adults will snap to attention. Young children must learn that their own needs do not *always* come first – sometimes they may have to be bored, or to wait when they don't want to, or to defer to the needs of others.

Learning to talk involves developing the physical muscles in and around the mouth, which allow us to make sounds. Language is learned rather than genetic – babies are born with the ability to *speak any language.* The language they speak (and the accent they use) will depend on the words they hear around them in those early weeks, months and years. The sounds and words are formed by using the tongue, teeth, lips, palate and vocal chords. The more parents and other people talk to and with a baby/young child, the quicker the child learns to speak. Research has also shown that children who are talked to frequently and in a high quality manner, will develop a higher IQ.

Speaking is intrinsically linked to hearing. Babies and young children hear others, and then try to emulate the patterns of speech and what other people say. This is why young children are given a hearing test to pick up issues – hearing problems can very quickly become language ones. As a practitioner working with young children, you should be on the look out for signs that a child's hearing might not be working properly. The symptoms below might point to issues with hearing:

✓ A child who doesn't respond when you call her name, especially if her back is turned to you;

✓ A child who appears to daydream a lot, and often doesn't seem to have listened properly to instructions;
✓ A child who talks very loudly;
✓ A child who mispronounces lots of different words;
✓ A child who seems grumpy or frustrated a lot of the time.

Developing complex talk patterns

Spoken language is actually full of rules, although we're not really aware that we are following these when we talk. As children learn to speak, they very quickly add grammatical constructs to what they are saying. Those first few words – 'dadda', 'mamma', 'ball' – are nouns, but the child very quickly adds verbs to the mix – 'mamma get ball' – and then pronouns – 'mummy get me the ball'. Amazingly, from about 3 years onwards, children can even adapt the way that they speak so that it's appropriate to the situation. For instance using different speech patterns with a friend of their own age than they do with a grown up.

It's important for you to be aware of the normal pattern of early speech development, so that you can spot any signs that a child might be having problems. You can download a copy of the table given below from the companion website.

Typical development of speech

TYPICAL DEVELOPMENT OF SPEECH
Young babies (pre-linguistic stage)
Makes eye contact with those who are speaking
Uses facial expressions to interact with others
Uses noises to communicate emotions
12 months plus
Uses one or more words
Points to something and names it
18 months plus
Learns up to 10 new words a day
Puts two or three word sentences together
Starts to use some grammatical constructions

⇨

Cont'd.

TYPICAL DEVELOPMENT OF SPEECH

2 years plus
Learns new words very quickly
Starts to include pronouns – I, me, you
Starts to string nouns and verbs together into sentences
Begins to use plurals
Uses questions frequently

3 years plus
People other than parents can understand speech
Begins to hold sustained conversations
Adapts tone, speech patterns and words depending on who she is talking with
Says his name and his age
Talks to herself while she plays

4 years plus
Extensive vocabulary
Can narrate a sequence of events ('First we . . ., then we . . .')
Uses language with his peers to share, take turns, squabble
Starts to use language to describe other people's emotions (empathy)
Lots of questions
Speaking clearly understandable, with very few mistakes

5 years plus
Creates well constructed sentences
Has a very wide vocabulary
Can offer her opinions during a discussion

6 years plus
Has a vocabulary of 10,000 words or more
Understands and can name opposites
Can use language to sort and classify in different ways (e.g. by colour, by shape)

7 years plus
Has a vocabulary of 20,000 words or more
Can use language to talk about the passing of time (days, weeks, seasons)

Learning how to listen

Learning how to communicate is as much about learning how to listen, as it is about learning how to talk. Children learn to speak through imitating what they hear other people say. If they don't listen (or can't hear) properly, then they will not learn to speak as effectively. Turn listening into a specific skill that you talk about, and which you practice in your setting. Have plenty of visual displays about listening around your setting, and plenty of opportunities for children to practice their listening throughout the day.

When you're working with a whole group or class, for instance introducing a new topic, incorporate 'talk partners'. When you ask a question of the whole group, give the children a minute or so to talk to a partner about what they think/feel/know. That way, the children get plenty of chance to practice both speaking *and* listening. You might also have 'chat buddies' or 'conversation buddies' – moments when you encourage the children to engage in sustained social chatting with their friends. A good time to do this might be at a snack time or just before break.

* * *

Practical project – Talking about listening

You will need

- A carpet or circle time session.

Learning intentions

- To encourage the children to think about what 'good listening' means;
- To improve focus, concentration and motivation to listen well;
- To enhance learning generally, through focusing on listening behaviour.

Instructions

During a carpet or circle time session, talk about 'good listening behaviour' with your children. Your key questions might include:

- ✓ How can we tell if someone is listening to us?
- ✓ Why do we need to sit still and keep our hands and feet to ourselves when we are on the carpet?
- ✓ What should we do if we want to ask something, or to answer a question?
- ✓ Why shouldn't we talk when someone else is speaking?

Your children's responses might include:

- ✓ How can we tell if someone is listening to us?
  - *If they are looking at us and making eye contact as we speak. If they can answer simple questions about what we were saying.*

✓ Why do we need to sit still and keep our hands and feet to ourselves when we are on the carpet?
  – *So that other children don't get distracted and can focus on
    what the teacher is saying. So that we don't bother or upset
    anyone else. So that we share the space equally.*

✓ What should we do if we want to ask something, or to answer
  a question?
  – *We should put up a hand so the teacher/practitioner knows
    we want to say something.*

✓ Why shouldn't we talk when someone else is speaking?
  – *Because it is rude. Because we won't be able to hear what
    they are saying. Because we should take turns.*

You'll find more on creating rules about listening and noise levels in
Signpost 3 – 'I can focus, concentrate and behave'.

*   *   *

Activities for listening

Designate specific times during your day when the children will practice
their listening. Having these quiet times is a great discipline, and is also
calming and relaxing, particularly for younger children. For instance
you might:

- Use a soundtrack on a listening centre to identify different animal noises;
- Listen to a recording of different bird songs; go outside to see if
  you can identify any specific birds;
- Have a variety of old telephones (children especially love the 'old
  style' handsets with a dial/receiver), for conversations in role play
  shops, offices, etc;
- Go on a 'listening walk' around your local area – you could
  record the sounds that you hear to listen to later;
- Get the group to practise being completely silent for increasing
  lengths of time, using a 'statues' or 'sleeping lions' type game.

Holding language in my head

When they reach the point of learning to write full sentences, your children will need to be able to hold that sentence in their heads, before they
write it down. Those children who struggle to do this will often turn into

children with very poor punctuation skills, because they don't under-stand where one sentence ends and another begins. You can help them develop punctuation skills at an early stage, so making it easier for them to do this later on. When you ask a question of the whole group, encour-age all the children to hold an answer in their heads. Depending on the age and confidence of the group, you might use a random method of choosing children to answer (names on lolly sticks). If there are quiet or shy children in the group, you could use 'talk partners', asking everyone to say their answer to the person next to them. Alternatively, all the chil-dren could call out their answer simultaneously, or for older children, write their answer on a whiteboard.

Practitioner talk

You, and your colleagues, are the most valuable resource that your early years setting or primary school can possibly offer the children. And one of the most valuable things that you can give to those children is high quality talk, discussion and conversation. When you're talking to a child, ensure that she can see your face, so that she can watch and copy the movements that you make as you form the sounds. Use your eyes to engage and interest the children, and your tone of voice to keep them focused and engaged.

It can sometimes take a while for children to form a word or sen-tence, or to finish what they are saying. Don't rush the child, or jump in before he has finished. Show instead that you are interested and willing to wait – demonstrate that his talk is important to you. Say to him: 'Gosh, that's really interesting, I wish I'd been there' when he's finished telling you his news.

Mistakes in speech

In the early years, children will often say words incorrectly, or have trouble making certain sounds. Where a child makes mistakes in his speech, for instance saying a word incorrectly, don't criticize the child and point out his error. Instead, simply repeat the word back to him, said or pronounced correctly. If a child makes repeated errors, or continues to mispronounce a letter or letter combination over a long period of time, refer him for a speech and language assessment. There may be a physical problem with his speech that can be addressed by some specialist intervention.

Why what you say matters

What you say, that is the actual words that you use, play an important part in helping your children become adept and confident communicators. Take care to praise effort over achievement – this has been shown to be the best way to motivate children to try harder and to achieve the highest expectations. Be specific about what you say, particularly when praising a child for doing something well. So, instead of saying:

> 'That's a really great painting, Tommy, you're such a good artist. Aren't you a clever boy!'

You might say:

> 'Wow, I can see that you've worked really hard on your painting Tommy. You really stuck at it. I love the way you've used red to show the volcano spurting out lava.'

I've spent a lot of time observing teachers and early years practitioners, and one very common habit is to constantly mention the gender of the child – saying 'good girl'/'good boy' all the time. Often, you won't even be aware that you're actually doing this. Try to avoid specifying gender all the time, because this suggests that what you say is based solely on whether the child is a boy or a girl, rather than a unique and interesting individual.

You might also find yourself using specific vocabulary depending on whether you are talking to or about a boy/girl (strong, boisterous vs pretty, silly). Both of these are very easy linguistic habits to fall into, and they can be hard to overcome. You'd be surprised how often practitioners and teachers do this, often without any realization of what they are doing.

Instead of saying:

> 'Tommy, stop being a silly boy and sit down now.'

You might say:

> *'Tommy, I need you to sit down right away, thanks.'*

Most of the time, you should talk as properly to the children as you can rather than mirroring their speech. 'Baby talk' has its occasional use for comforting very young children if they get upset, but most of the time you should model 'proper' speech for your children. That's not to say you should be using very complicated, adult terminology. But if you only ever use very simple vocabulary, your children will have no chance to learn more complex words and grammatical constructions. The secret is to drip feed new words slowly, all the time checking for comprehension.

If a child makes a mistake with his vocabulary, model the correct word for him, rather than highlighting his mistake. So, if a child says:

> *'I builded it.'*

You might say . . .

> *'Yes, you built it, well done!'*

Similarly, if a child mispronounces a word ('lellow' instead of 'yellow', which is a very common mistake), repeat the word pronounced properly, but without highlighting the mistake that has been made.

Introducing new vocabulary

Be aware that, all the time, you are introducing new vocabulary into your children's worlds. Use talk to show the children how you can say the same thing in different ways, and using different vocabulary. Have a kind of 'running commentary' of talk for your children to hear, particularly when you are playing alongside them. For instance when talking about a tower that a child is building, you might use or introduce a huge variety of words:

> *'tall, taller, tallest, high, higher, highest, tower, towering, skyscraper, build, built, building, construct, construction, structure, strong, weak'*

Develop the vocabulary of mark making with your children as well. Make sure you use words such as:

> 'line, draw, write, scribble, doodle, note, jot down, mark, record, note down, list, register'

Why *how* you say what you say matters

There are several key reasons why tone (how you say what you say) is vital:

- Not all of your children will understand all of your vocabulary, all of the time;
- This is especially so if you teach children who have English as an additional language, or if you work with very young children or babies;
- Not all of your children will be listening to every single one of your words all of the time;
- However, they will tune in to your general emotional state through the sound of your voice (or 'prosody');
- Tone helps children understand the meaning, and also the context, of the language we use;
- Tone cues us in to social information – if you sound sarcastic, or superior, or interested, or warm, this gives them clues about you as a person.

Interestingly, the parts of the brain which are connected to emotion are also stimulated by our use of vocal tone. In other words, if I sound happy, this stimulates the part of your brain that processes emotion, and you feel happy too. Remember, you don't have to actually *be* happy or excited to *sound* happy or excited. As a practitioner or teacher this is one of the key skills that you can use to enhance communication – adding warmth, variety and 'music' to the way that you sound.

* * *

Practical project – Communicating through tone

You will need

- A staff training day;
- Several teachers/practitioners.

Learning intentions

- To help practitioners develop their use of tone when speaking with children;
- To show that *how* you say something matters a great deal.

Instructions

Divide your staff up into pairs. One person will be the child, the other person will be the adult. The child is playing, the practitioner is asking questions or giving encouragement. The staff can *only* use consecutive numbers to communicate – as few or as many at a time as they wish. For instance the first person might say '1, 2, 3', the second '4', the first '5, 6', then the second '7, 8, 9, 10'.

The idea is to communicate, and have a clearly understandable conversation, through the use of vocal tone alone. Someone watching should be able to 'tell' what the conversation is about. If your staff are brave enough, they could show their role plays to the rest of the group to see if what they are saying can be translated.

*   *   *

Imaginative talk

Young children respond very well to talk that appears to come from an inanimate object, such as a toy or a puppet. Engaging in these pretend 'conversations' is a great way to support their imaginative development. Using a puppet can encourage your children to talk more freely than they might to an adult. Talking through a puppet can also encourage you to put aside your inhibitions and be more creative in the way that you speak with your children.

Language delay

Most children don't just naturally 'grow out of' language problems. It's vital for the children in your care that you identify any issues early on, and organize intervention to help them develop their language skills. A month of intervention in the early years, can be the equivalent to six months input later on. If you find it hard to understand what a child is saying, particularly by the age of 3 years, then it is likely that there is some kind of issue with his language development. The younger the child, the more impact an intervention has; so it is vital to flag up any concerns you have sooner rather than later. A highly experienced language therapist that I met recently suggested that the window of opportunity for resolving language issues closes when the child is about five and a half years old.

Remember, too, that a child with language delay will be impacted in several other areas of his learning and development. He will find it harder to socialize and make friends because he can't join in easily with games or with conversations. He will also find it harder to learn at the same rate as his peers, and will almost certainly read and write later than is normal for his age. Sometimes, the child will have a special need (such as being on the autistic spectrum, or having attention deficit disorder), which impacts on several areas of his development – language, socialization, behaviour, learning.

There are a variety of different reasons why a child's language development might be delayed – sometimes related to hearing, but not always. Remember that hearing issues can develop *after* a hearing test has been given, and that testing and diagnosis can be patchy. In some areas young children have their hearing and language development checked several times, in other areas this does not happen at all. A child could have language delay because of:

- An undiagnosed hearing impairment;
- Delayed oral motor development (i.e. development of the muscles needed for speech has not happened properly);
- Issues with the brain or central nervous system;
- Issues with physical, psychological or intellectual development;
- Social and emotional issues;
- Specific special needs, such as being on the autistic spectrum.

It is your duty as an early years practitioner or teacher to highlight any concerns you have, and to explain to parents why it's so important to identify and treat language delay early on. Parents may react negatively to being told that their child has what is perceived as a 'problem'. Make sure that you share information about language development with them, and explain how positive the outcomes can be for the child where early intervention does take place.

*　＊　＊*

Practical project – Providing a parent/carer workshop

You will need

- Several teachers/practitioners to present/run activities;
- An audience of interested parents;
- A computer/laptop, data projector and screen;
- Resources for several different language activities you do at your setting.

Learning intentions

- To help parents understand more about how language develops;
- To encourage parents to understand what language delay is;
- To encourage parents to support communication, language and literacy at home.

Find useful resources to support your parent workshop in the companion website

- The PowerPoint presentation we used at our preschool for the parent workshop;
- A leaflet we created to hand out to parents to take away with them.

Instructions

Host a parent workshop based around communication, language and literacy. At our preschool, we did this in response to questions from parents about 'why aren't you teaching them to write properly' (i.e. to sit and trace over their names). We felt it was clear that parents needed more information about how young children actually learn to write. We were also concerned about the number of children who were coming into our setting with weak language skills.

In our workshop we used some PowerPoint slides, as well as some quick challenges for parents (how many words would a child know at different ages?), and also some activities for them to do with their children. For instance writing 'letters' and posting them in our postbox, and also fine motor activities such as threading and weaving.

*   *   *

I'm Physically Able to Make Marks

2

In this section . . .

- Help your children build up their muscle strength – both fine and gross motor skills
- Encourage your children to develop their dexterity
- Increase your children's eye to hand coordination
- Help your children develop a correct pencil grip

Consider this . . .

Children develop the ability to control their bodies from the centre of the body outwards, and from the head downwards. In other words, a small baby gradually strengthens her neck muscles, until she can hold her head upright. After learning to roll over and sit, she builds up her strength until she can crawl and then walk. Once a child is walking, she must build up strength in her whole body before she can balance herself to sit and write. Similarly, a child learns first to control her shoulder and whole arm movements before she can control her hands and fingers. As she develops her fine motor control, she will eventually learn how to make the grip and the very fine movements that are needed to hold a pencil and write.

Writing takes a surprising amount of hand and finger strength – think about how your hands ache when you have to handwrite for a long time, for instance in an exam. It's also important that the child has sufficient body strength to maintain a good posture when sitting to write. At this stage in their development, your children need to build up their whole body, hand and finger strength through a variety of different activities. As well as building strength and control of their muscular movements, children also need to learn to coordinate – to create those eye to hand connections within the brain that are required for writing.

Often the activities you use to achieve these gross and fine motor skills will appear to have nothing to do with 'mark making' or 'writing' as an adult might view it. However, they all contribute to your children being able to write, and write neatly, in the future. Share information with parents about how and why these activities are so important for young children, so that they understand the approaches you use in your setting, and also what they can do to support their child at home. Ask parents not to push their children to 'hold a pencil and write properly' before they are ready. This can do more damage than good, particularly if the child does not have the muscular strength needed to hold a pencil correctly.

Building whole body strength

In order to be able to sit down and make marks, a child must first be able to support his trunk in an upright position, and keep his head well supported. This requires a good sense of balance, strength in the stomach muscles and also in the neck and shoulders. An incorrect writing posture, or a posture in which the child supports himself by leaning on the furniture, will in turn lead to problems later on in the child's school career.

As well as developing muscular tone, physical activities help children build skills such as coordination and concentration, and are important for healthy development in general. Aim to get your children using cross body movements, which encourage the development of right brain/left brain connections. Your gross motor activities might include:

✓ Balance beams;
✓ Balance on one leg for a set time;
✓ Obstacle courses with cones;
✓ Crawling through tunnels;
✓ Building and hiding in dens;
✓ Target practice;
✓ Climbing frames and slides;
✓ Ride on toys;

✓ Balance bikes;
✓ Running races;
✓ Skipping;
✓ Spinning hoops;
✓ Throwing and catching activities;
✓ Hop Scotch;
✓ Different ways of walking – on tiptoes, forwards, backwards, sideways;
✓ Digging in a garden area;
✓ Carrying buckets of water/sand;
✓ Dance sessions;
✓ Yoga sessions;
✓ Wheelbarrow walking;
✓ Tug of war (with supervision);
✓ Trips to a local park or play area;
✓ Monkey bars (if you have access to these, they are wonderful for grip strength as well).

Hand press starter activity

This exercise is great for hand, arm and upper body strength, and develops lots of the most important muscles concerned with mark making and writing. It works well as a starter activity before doing some writing:

✓ Get the children to stand in a space;
✓ Ask them to put their hands out in front of them, palms together (in a similar position to that of someone praying);
✓ Now get the children to push their palms together hard – they should feel the muscles in their arms, shoulders and upper body working;
✓ Hold for 5 seconds and then release;
✓ Repeat several times, building up the amount of repetitions each time you do this activity.

Bilateral integration – crossing the mid line

Most people have one side of their body which is dominant – for most of us, this is the right hand (and also the right foot, right eye and so on). When we pick up a pen that is to our left, we reach for it with our right hand, across the centre or mid line of our bodies. However, even though one side is dominant, we are able to get the two sides of our bodies to work together efficiently. Otherwise, we would not be able to do activities such as tying a knot or clapping our hands. When kicking a ball with our dominant right leg, the other leg helps balance and support our body.

Writing requires the ability to coordinate the two sides of our body – the left hand holds the paper while the right hand holds the writing tool. Similarly, we must be able to cross the midline, keeping the pen in our right hand as we move across the page, rather than swapping it from left to right at the midpoint. Those children who struggle with this bilateral integration will often also struggle with both reading and writing. Encourage your children to practise 'crossing the midline' activities, to help them develop this skill.

As well as learning how to use the two sides of their bodies together, it's also important for children to practise what is known as 'asymmetrical bilateral integration'. In other words, moving the two sides of the body simultaneously, but in opposite directions (as a baby does when she crawls). The Brain Gym® activities which have become very popular in schools in recent years encourage this cross laterality. Help your children learn to get the two sides of their brains working together to coordinate the body and to improve their cognitive functioning.

✓ Play Simon says – with your instructions requiring the children to cross the midline (e.g. touch your left shoulder with your right hand);

✓ Get the children to tap their heads, and pat their stomachs at the same time;

✓ Ask the children to put their right hand on the left side of their nose, and their left hand on their right cheek, and then swap the two over;

✓ Set up an obstacle course with lots of tunnels, through which the children must crawl;

✓ Offer a small stepladder for your children to climb, and show them how to do it using cross lateral movements;

✓ Encourage them to kick a football with their non dominant (usually the left) foot.

Poor motor skills

There are a number of reasons why a child might have poor motor skills. It could be that she lives in an area where there are few opportunities for outdoor play. Perhaps there are no parks locally, or maybe her parents feel it is unsafe for her to play outside because of a main road. Perhaps he watches a great deal of television, or he has been unwell or not allowed to play outside because of overprotective parents. It may be that he has some kind of specific motor difficulties or sensory processing disorder.

Dyspraxia

This is a term for a child who has special needs involving his motor skills – he finds it hard to organize his movements. Typically, a child with dyspraxia may appear clumsy, slow and easily distracted. He will need help to develop movement skills that other children grasp instinctively. Parents of a child who has dyspraxia might have noticed that their child was slow to reach the normal developmental milestones, particularly those to do with movement. Of course, writing is a skill that requires high levels of *control* of movement, so a child who has dyspraxia will struggle to pick up this particular skill.

As with all special needs, early identification is the key. Keep an eye out for the following problems which may indicate that a child in your setting has dyspraxia, and will need additional support to access all aspects of education:

- Finds it particularly hard to stay still;
- Tends to speak more loudly than is needed;
- Bumps into things, falls over frequently;
- Tends not to participate in imaginative and creative play;
- Finds it hard to judge levels of risk of physical activities (e.g. jumps from height);
- Flaps hands when running;
- Is a messy eater;
- Is isolated from his peers;
- Has poor language development;
- Finds it hard to concentrate.

Children who have dyspraxia will find it hard to deal with an open plan area, and with high levels of visual stimulation (for instance displays hanging down from the ceiling). They will also struggle with independent skills, such as getting dressed. You can help by suggesting to parents that they give the child shoes/clothes which are easy to put on (e.g. Velcro straps on shoes).

Supporting children with dyspraxia

There are plenty of strategies you can put in place, to help a child in your setting who has dyspraxia. Look first at the environment itself – avoid strip lights and over busy walls. By minimizing sensory distractions, you will encourage the child to feel more settled and relaxed. Choose activities which aid the development of motor skills, but support the child one-to-one, ensuring that you help him break down the skills into manageable chunks. You might:

- ✓ Offer plenty of chances to practise balance and aim – wobble boards, walking on a straight line, throwing at or into a target area;
- ✓ Give the child a visual timetable, so that she learns about what your routines are and how the day is structured;
- ✓ Use visual prompts to help the child understand what the activities are, and what he should do next;
- ✓ Have a 'time out' option that the child can use if she is feeling stressed and needs a break.

Building hand and finger strength

Our fingers and hands play a vital role in our day-to-day lives, helping us to perform many tasks and actions such as grasping, pointing, feeling, writing, drawing, stroking, picking up, climbing and so on. About a quarter of the motor cortex in your brain (the part of the brain which controls all body movement) is dedicated to the movement of your hands. Interestingly, we use many of the muscles in the lower arm to control our finger movements, as well as those smaller muscles within the hands.

Your children will naturally develop their hand and finger strength during the course of their normal daily routine (brushing their teeth, pulling on clothes). Encourage your children to be as independent as possible – only help them if really necessary, for instance encouraging them to try to do up their coats by themselves. You can also help your children develop strength through specific exercises and activities. When referring to hand and finger strength in relation to mark making, you should aim to develop your children's:

✓ Grip strength (i.e. their whole hand strength);
✓ Pinch strength (i.e. the strength of the thumb and forefinger and sometimes the middle finger as well).

Those children who don't have good control of their hands and fingers will not be able to gather the very subtle sensory information that is needed to make marks with a pencil. What tends to happen is that these children over compensate for the lack of control and feeling in their fingers, and end up grasping the mark making tools very tightly. Below you'll find a wide variety of activities designed to help your children build their hand and finger strength.

Activities for snack or lunch time

✓ Get the children involved in preparing foods – grating, chopping or cutting up foods for snack time, or in a cookery session;
✓ Squeeze oranges to make juice to have with their snacks;
✓ Have jugs on the tables, so that children can pour their own drinks (and a cloth for mopping up any messes – squeezing out cloths is great for hand strength too);
✓ Wipe their own mats or tables after eating.

Activities with sand and water

✓ Put items in your water tray that the children can squeeze – squashy toys, foam sponges, etc;
✓ Pour liquids from a large jug into a small one, or from a jug into a cup;

✓ Use a jug with measuring lines on it, and get the children to aim to pour up to a specific line;

✓ Carry heavy buckets filled with water or sand;

✓ Squeeze wet sand together to make 'sand balls' (and fresh snow in the water tray to make snow balls whenever you get the chance);

✓ Wash up toy plates in washing up water, with a cloth, either in a role play kitchen sink, in a water tray or in a real sink;

Drawing and writing activities

✓ Offer your children chances to draw on a vertical surface – an easel, or some paper attached to the wall. This develops more hand and wrist strength than drawing on a horizontal surface;

✓ Give lots of chances to trace a line to find the right way through a maze – both small-scale and on large paper;

✓ Ask for help in sharpening the pencils for you;

✓ Get the children to hang up paintings (or 'washing') to dry with some pegs.

Squashing and squishing activities

✓ Offer the children different malleable materials to knead, squeeze and play with – play dough, clay, pastry, gloop, sand, mud;

✓ Roll small pieces of clay or play dough up into tiny balls (perhaps to make 'peas' for a doll's dinner);

✓ Scrunch up balls of newspaper and throw them into a basket;

✓ Get the children to regularly squash a soft ball – build up repetitions gradually – first ten, then twenty and so on;

✓ Move on to using a tennis ball as hand strength increases;

✓ Give the children bubble wrap to pop;

✓ Crush a whole sheet of newspaper, using only one hand (this is a good activity for older children).

Sports games and activities

✓ Face a partner, put your palms together, now push against each other;

✓ Play a game of tug of war with a soft cord or rope;

✓ Squash a meat baster to blow ping pong balls around an obstacle course;
✓ Get the children to do 'finger push-ups', seeing how many times they can open a peg in succession.

Activities with toys/objects

✓ Use pop together and pull apart toys – these are particularly good for developing pinch strength.
✓ Fill some plastic jars with interesting objects – stars, crystals, beads, small toy animals. Encourage the children to unscrew the jar, tip out the objects, return the objects to the jar and then screw it up again.
✓ Use tongs or tweezers to pick up small toys or beads and put them into a bowl. Add a competitive element by seeing how many they can do in 1 minute.
✓ Carry shopping bags in a supermarket role play area.
✓ Put coins into a piggy bank.
✓ Sort various natural objects into different pots – stones, leaves, acorns, etc.
✓ Turn keys to lock and unlock a door.

* * *

Practical project – At the garage

You will need

- Several ride on cars and other vehicles;
- Water squirters (the kind used for misting plants work well);
- Cloths and sponges;
- Buckets or bowls of water;
- Outdoor chalks;
- Clipboards and pencils;
- Tools (real, as appropriate, or toy ones);
- Large blocks or crates (to raise up cars for repair);
- Tills, telephones, other office equipment.

Learning intentions

- To help your children build hand and finger strength, in preparation for writing;
- To encourage the children to practise their eye to hand coordination;
- To use a garage setting particularly to inspire the boys to make marks.

Instructions

Set up part of your outdoor area or playground as a 'garage'. You can do this ahead of time, or get your children involved in deciding how they would like to lay out the various areas. The mark making activities they can do at their garage include:

- ✓ Marking out 'bays' for the cars, with outdoor chalks;
- ✓ Taking customer details on clipboards when they drop off their cars;
- ✓ Washing the cars with squirters to build hand/finger strength;
- ✓ Squeezing out sponges and cloths (again this builds hand strength);
- ✓ Repairing the cars with tools (this builds dexterity);
- ✓ Working in the office area – taking phone bookings, or payments for repairs.

* * *

Developing dexterity

When we talk about dexterity, what we really mean are those very fine small motor skills involving the use of the fingers. The more dexterous a child becomes, the better able he will be to form letters correctly when he comes to write. As well as fine motor skills, dexterity often requires a high level of focus and concentration, as the child's brain forms the connections required to make the hand move in a certain way and to a certain place (see the section on 'Eye to hand coordination' below for more on this). The following activities will all help you increase your children's dexterity:

- ✓ Tearing up paper;
- ✓ Cutting up paper with a pair of scissors;
- ✓ Threading with beads;
- ✓ Using tweezers to pick up small items;
- ✓ Using chopsticks, for instance to pick up noodles;
- ✓ Writing with quills;
- ✓ Doing up buttons and zips;
- ✓ Putting shoes on independently;
- ✓ Using hole and paper punches;
- ✓ Using staplers;
- ✓ Putting paper clips on paper (far trickier than you'd imagine – see the photo);
- ✓ Playing with wind up toys;

✓ Using sellotape or masking tape to make pictures, to wrap things up, or to join things together.

In the photo below you can see Niamh putting a paperclip onto a piece of paper, in our writing area. Notice the high level of concentration she displays, and the fine finger movements she's using, as she completes this activity. (You might also notice that Niamh is left-handed.)

* * *

✋ Practical project – Happy birthday to you!

You will need

- A variety of different sized boxes;
- Sellotape, preferably in child-friendly dispensers;
- Several pairs of scissors;
- A selection of different kinds of wrapping paper;
- A selection of string, ribbons and other decorative items;
- Birthday cards and envelopes.

Learning intentions

- To help the children develop dexterity and fine motor skills;
- To practise using a pair of scissors to cut accurately;
- To use a writing tool and write for a purpose.

Instructions

This activity is great for encouraging the children to use their fingers and develop their dexterity. Get your children to wrap presents and write cards for a real person (mum, dad, a friend) or a fictional character's birthday. Offer a selection of different kinds of boxes, pre-cut paper, rolls of wrapping paper and ribbons, as well as different birthday cards and envelopes. If you don't have a sellotape dispenser, cut short lengths of sellotape and put them along the side of a table, for the children to pinch off and use.

* * *

In the photo below you can see Matty enjoying our Birthday activity and taking great care in writing a birthday card for his friend.

Moving individual fingers

As well as activities where the children are required to 'pinch' their fingers together, encourage your children to learn how to move their fingers separately. You can do this by:

✓ Using songs such as 'Ten Little Fishes' where the fingers hide or disappear. Find a link which gives lots of examples of number songs in the companion website;
✓ Using finger and hand puppets, for instance to retell a story;
✓ Playing on a keyboard or piano;
✓ Making shadow puppets using fingers and torches within a darkened tent;
✓ Making drawings in different substances (mud, sand, paint) using their finger tips, particularly with the index finger.

Eye to hand coordination

In order to write the eyes must guide the hand to form the correct letter shapes, to stay on the line and within the page. Eye tracking skills are also vital for reading, so that the child can fix on and follow text along a page. This skill is sometimes referred to as eye to body coordination and, more technically, as 'visual-motor integration'. Many sports are based around the notion of good eye to hand coordination – tennis being a prime example.

Use gross motor activities to build strength and coordination, giving the children large resources to begin with (a large bat, a large ball, a big target). Gradually work with smaller and smaller resources, as the children become more accurate in their eye to hand/arm coordination. Incorporate plenty of opportunities for fine motor activities that build fine eye/hand coordination as well. Developing fine motor eye to hand coordination is particularly important for independent care activities such as getting dressed, doing up buttons and feeding oneself. You can find lots of ideas below to use to help your children develop their eye to hand coordination.

Gross motor activities for eye/hand coordination

✓ Playing catch with a ball in groups or with partners;
✓ Hitting a ball with a bat;

✓ Tossing a bean bag in the air and catching it;
✓ With several children standing in a row, getting them to pass a ball over their heads or through their legs;
✓ Using remote control and programmable toys, such as a Bee-bot, to encourage the children to follow an object with their eyes.

You can also try rolling a ball through a child's legs, as follows:

✓ Get the child to stand with his back to you, legs apart in a V shape;
✓ Now roll a small ball through his legs;
✓ As soon as he sees it appear, he must follow it with his eyes and then move to collect it.

Fine motor activities for eye/hand coordination

✓ Building towers with blocks;
✓ Putting pegs into a peg board;
✓ Threading beads onto a string;
✓ Cutting up food for snack time;
✓ Colouring in (this requires the child to control hand and arm muscles so they don't go over the lines);
✓ Icing biscuits;
✓ Placing Hama beads into a design on a Hama board (for very dextrous or older children);
✓ Playing a xylophone;
✓ Cutting or tearing paper, especially around an outline;
✓ Tracing between two lines, or through a maze, with a finger or with a pencil.

* * *

Practical project – Balloon 'Keepy Uppy'

You will need

● Balloons – at least one per child (have a few spares in case some pop);
● An open space – indoors is best as the wind makes this super tricky outside.

Learning intentions

● Building eye to hand coordination in a fun, safe way;
● Developing counting skills.

Instructions

Give each of your children a balloon. Explain that they must keep it up in the air for as long as possible, simply by tapping it upwards with their hands. You could do this all together, counting upwards as you go. Or, each child could have a go on her own.

Set a challenge to see whether the children can increase the number they do over a series of days or weeks, as their eye to hand coordination improves. They could even write the number they do on the balloon, to take home with them.

* ⋆ ⋆

Vision and eye/hand coordination

It stands to reason that, in order to coordinate the eyes to hand or body, children need to be able to see well. Even if a child has had his eyes tested, certain problems may not be picked up. While an eye test checks for clarity of vision, there are various other issues which may affect a child's ability to work with marks on a page. All of these problems can affect a child's ability to both read and write. They include:

- **Eye teaming problems** – this is where the child's eyes find it hard to aim at the same point on the page. When the brain reads the information coming from each eye it creates a blurred image. The child has to strain to try and stop the print from blurring.
- **Tracking problems** – to follow marks on a page, children must learn to track them. Children who have tracking problems struggle to control their eye movements at close range.
- **Focus problems** – school frequently requires children to focus at a distance (look at the board) and then change to focusing up close (write on the page). Children who have focus problems may suffer from frequent headaches.
- **Vision perception problems** – these are a variety of issues with giving meaning to what is seen, that is to perceiving marks on a page. For instance visual spatial orientation includes being able to perceive where your body is in relation to the world around you.

 Visit the companion website for a link to a useful website on this subject. If you have concerns about a child you work with, you will find a very helpful checklist of the symptoms of vision problems on this site.

Holding a mark making tool

The fact that we can hold a mark making tool and use it to communicate with each other via writing is a key part of what makes us human. The skill of holding and manoeuvring the tool takes time to develop – at first just scribbles, but gradually the letter shapes start to take form. By making it seem fun and natural to work with all kinds of different mark making tools, you give your children the chance to build up all the skills that they need to be able to write.

The role of drawing and painting

Drawing and painting are, of course, all forms of 'mark making', which help the child form letters at a later stage. (As well as, of course, being a skill and an art form in their own right.) At first, children don't differentiate between marks made to create a picture and marks made to convey meaning through words. Gradually, though, they learn to separate out their drawing from their 'writing'. Often, the first 'word' that they attempt to write spontaneously will be their names.

When it comes to painting, most children absolutely *love* to get messy. This is perhaps one of the key reasons why it is so important to offer painting as a part of the child's preschool, nursery or primary school experience. Quite a lot of parents shy away from doing much painting at home for fear of the mess that can result. In the more accommodating early years environment, we don't mind if a child covers his hands with paints to make hand prints (even though we might have intended him to use a paint brush!). Yes, it can lead to a very messy and stressful session but it offers huge rewards in terms of sensory experiences and the chance for creative expression.

You can have a lot of fun with drawing and painting while, at the same time, helping your children develop many of the skills they need to hold a mark making tool. Paint is a wonderfully sensory resource as well, and children absolutely love getting it on their hands, feet and, indeed, in their hair! You could try:

✓ Dipping marbles in paint, and getting the children to roll them around on paper to see what marks they create;

✓ Treading some toy dinosaurs in paint, to use as stampers, and creating trails of 'dinosaur footprints' across a page;

✓ Getting the children to tread in paint, and then walk across a long roll of paper;

✓ Painting with natural materials, such as long grasses. This activity is also brilliant for developing eye to hand coordination – it's tricky to get the grass in the paint and on the paper, let alone to control the marks that you make.

In the photograph below, you can see that the children have used various different methods to 'make their mark' on a long sheet of paper. Some used their hands, others used long grasses, others used a brush. This kind of group mark making activity is great fun, and the children inspire each other to experiment with different tools. By using a long sheet of lining paper, there is plenty of space for the children to make their own mark.

Talking about drawing

Children will often create a narrative as they draw or paint a picture, talking through what it is they are creating. Encourage your children to use drawing and painting alongside verbal expression – this both extends their vocabulary and helps them understand how narratives have a structure. Avoid imposing your own interpretation on a child's drawing – if you ask '*is that a dinosaur?*' the child may well just agree. Often, marks appear within children's drawings and paintings which are similar to letters. Gradually, they begin to understand that marks can hold meaning in the form of a word and they start to experiment with these.

Achieving a correct grasp

It's very tricky for small hands to achieve a correct 'adult style' pencil grasp. At first, young children of about 2–3 years will use a fist grip, preferably with a chunky pencil. This will usually develop into a finger grasp, perhaps one that uses all five fingers. All these grasps are inefficient for writing because it is the wrist that controls the pencil, rather than the fingers.

In the first photo below, you can see Niamh (who has just turned three) holding her pencil with a 'fist grip'.

In this second photo, Niamh is using more of a 'finger grasp' type grip.

Depending on the size, strength and ability of the individual child, she should be ready to start using a correct pencil grasp from about the age of 3 or 4 years old. As the child reaches school age, and is expected to write more frequently, it's particularly important to discourage her from using an incorrect grip. Once a poor habit takes hold it is very hard to break: even if it does not appear to disadvantage the child at this age, it may well cause difficulties with writing later on in the child's school career. Keep a close eye on your children as they become more confident about holding a pencil and as they begin to form letters. If you notice incorrect habits forming, for instance a child who continues to use a fist grip, intervene before the habit becomes ingrained. Those chunky pencil grips can help a child who is struggling to hold a pencil correctly.

The ideal is for children to develop a form of what is known as a 'dynamic tripod grasp' (sometimes also called the 'dynamic tripod grip'). With the 'dynamic tripod grasp':

✓ The pen or pencil is held between the thumb and the index and middle fingers;
✓ The child makes a 'tripod' shape with the thumb and fingers;

✓ The *fingers*, rather than the wrist, move the pencil;
✓ The hand and fingers are relaxed and a light pressure is exerted on the paper;
✓ The pencil rests comfortably on the web space between the thumb and index finger;
✓ The fingers and thumb form a 'C' shape, rather than the space being flattened out;
✓ The pencil is held with the tips of the thumb/fingers rather than in the joint of the thumb.

However, each child will develop his or her own particular style of 'tripod' grip, as you can see in the photos below.

In the first photo, Álvie (9 years old) is using a fairly mature, relaxed tripod grip and he is able to form his handwriting well, even under timed conditions.

In the second photo, Jack (6 years old, foreground) is using a relaxed tripod position, while Edite's (5 years old, background) index finger appears bent and tense. She has recently learned cursive writing, and is keen to write neatly. With time, her finger strength should improve and she should be able to relax her fingers more.

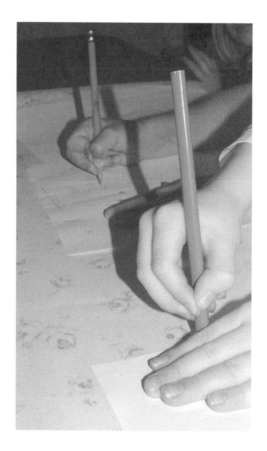

 Go to the companion website to find a link to a fascinating video extract from a workshop about pencil writing skills.

*   *   *

Practical project – The pencil olympics

You will need

- A child, group of children or whole class;
- A pencil for each child;
- A pair of chopsticks for each child;
- A pile of small objects, for instance paper clips or beads;
- A pot for each child.

Learning intentions

- To help the children develop their finger strength and dexterity;
- To check for any weaknesses or issues in individual children.

Instructions

Try hosting the 'pencil olympics' with your older or more dexterous children, or to check for issues in a whole class of writers.

Event One: Ask the children to hold their pencils using a Dynamic Tripod Grasp. Now, they must move the pencil along between their fingers until they are holding it by the end, moving up and down the length of the pencil and just using the tips of the fingers.

Event Two: Now, holding the pencil between the index and middle fingers, ask the children to twirl the 'baton' around and around, again just using the tips of the fingers.

Event Three: Finally, each child should take a pair of chopsticks, again holding them using a Dynamic Tripod Grasp. Now, they should pick up as many of the small objects as they can and place them in their pots, using the chopsticks.

*   *   *

Supporting children who are left-handed

Hand preference tends to be fixed after about 3 years of age, and between 8 and 15 per cent of the world's population will have a preference for using their left hand. Very few people are genuinely ambidextrous, although some people may use different hands for different activities. For those children whose preference is to use their left hand, this has the potential to cause difficulties, particularly when it comes to mark making and writing. You need to be aware of the issues which may arise, and work to pre-empt or overcome them. This might be through the resources that you offer, or through the way that you set up activities.

A child who is left-handed will have to *pull* the writing tool across the page, rather than *pushing* it as a right hander does. The child will also cover her marks as she moves along the line, potentially smudging what she has written and also making it harder to retain the sense of what she is writing. Some people who are left-handed will develop a kind of 'hooked' posture, whereby they hook their hand over their writing (so that they can see what they are doing as they write). However, by helping the child adopt the correct posture and writing position when they first learn to write, you can avoid this.

Here are some top tips for supporting children who are left-handed:

- ✓ Present all mark making activities at the child's midline, rather than to one side – this will help your children decide for themselves on their hand preference.
- ✓ It is easier for left-handed children to write on a slope, so offer them an easel or a raised surface.
- ✓ It is also a very good idea to give left-handed children chances to do large-scale mark making, so that they don't always feel that their hand is getting in the way of what they wanted to write or draw.
- ✓ Advise a child who is left-handed to hold the pencil below the writing as they write, so that they can see what they are doing.
- ✓ Encourage the child to tilt the paper at about 45 degrees clockwise, so that the top of the page tilts slightly to the right.
- ✓ Show the child how to hold the pencil at about 2.5 to 3.8 cm away from the tip – this will help him see what he is writing.
- ✓ Watch the child as she writes to make sure that she doesn't begin to adopt an awkward posture.
- ✓ Minimize pressure on the child to write, as she may end up using an over-tight grip to try and write 'neatly'.
- ✓ Watch where you sit the child. Make sure that they are to the left of any right-handers, so that the two children do not bump elbows as they write.
- ✓ When left-handed children are learning letter formation, remember that it is fine to slope letters to the left, as well as to the right. (If you're right-handed, you may need to overcome your instinctive feeling that this is 'wrong'.)
- ✓ Remember that letter formation is slightly different for children who are left-handed (see below for an internet link for more on this).

Check also whether you have a left-handed pair of scissors on offer in your setting. If not, your left-handed children will struggle to cut as well as they might. When a child who is left-handed cuts with right-handed scissors, they have to hold them in an awkward way, and this will be uncomfortable for the child. Don't be fooled by 'both ways' pairs of scissors, which claim to be suitable for both right and left-handed children. These pairs of scissors have a grip which works both ways, but the blade is still the 'wrong' way for your left-handers. With a left-handed pair of scissors, the left blade is kept on top, so that the children can see where they are cutting as the pair of scissors moves through the paper.

In the photo below you can see Alex enjoying some large-scale outdoor mark making with his left hand.

Mirror writing

Some very famous left-handed people such as Leonardo da Vinci used mirror writing. If you notice that a child is starting to write his letters backwards and back to front in this way, encourage him to start writing from the left hand side of the page. Tracing over words (with arrows to indicate direction) can also be a helpful strategy to overcome this.

See the companion website for a link to a very useful site all about 'handedness', and which gives advice on how to teach left-handed children to write. You can also find a link to a site which gives letter formation instructions for children who are left-handed.

Mark making and posture

As we've seen right from the start of this book, in order to control our writing, we must first be able to control our bodies. Those children who do not have good muscle strength in their trunks will find it hard to write neatly. Indeed, they will find it hard to sit at a seat with good posture for any length of time. Watch out for the telltale signs of poorly developed stomach muscles – these will be the children who:

- Slump or flop over onto the table when they are writing;
- Lean with their stomachs against the table;
- Use their elbows to support their bodies;
- Wrap their legs around the chair or table to gain balance;
- Walk with their tummies sticking out, rather than their tails 'tucked under'.

These children will need your support to build up their gross motor strength before they can hope to hold the correct posture for writing.

Correct posture for writing

Your children will spend a good proportion of the next ten years or more of their lives writing while seated at a desk. It's therefore vital that they learn to sit properly and, indeed, that they have the muscular strength to sit properly. An incorrect posture can often lead to an incorrect pencil grasp, and also to issues with back and neck pain. If you stop for a moment and think about your own posture when you write, you will probably be aware that you've picked up some bad habits over time. (As I type this I'm aware that my legs are crossed and my back is slumped – at least I do have an adjustable chair and my elbows are at the right angle.)

The ideal is for your children to achieve what is known as a '90–90–90' position. In other words, a body shape with three 90 degree angles:

- ✓ Feet flat on floor with a 90 degree angle at the ankles;
- ✓ Knees bent at 90 degrees;
- ✓ Arms flat on the table with a 90 degree angle at the elbows.

Where possible, help your children achieve a seating position where the chair is the correct height in relation to the table, so that the lower arms are not tilted up or down and the elbows are roughly in line with the waist. Typically, the furniture in schools is not specifically adjustable to children of different ages and heights. So, this might mean offering cushions for smaller children, or, if you can, tables at a variety of heights.

In addition to sustaining the correct posture, you should also encourage your children to stabilize their paper with the non-dominant hand, that is to keep it still with the left hand if they are right-handed, and vice versa for the children who are left-handed.

I Can Concentrate, Focus and Behave

In this section . . .

- Help your children develop control of their impulses
- Encourage your children to make good choices about learning
- Develop effective rules, structures and rewards for behaviour
- Help your children to build their focus and pay attention for longer periods of time
- Understand the link between concentration and writing ability

Consider this . . .

Writing is inextricably linked to behaviour; if a child cannot stay in his seat, focus on the task or have the patience to practice and persevere, his writing will inevitably be poor. Children need to learn to listen, to focus, to pay attention and to be self-disciplined, if they are to get the best out of their schooling. So much of education relies on the ability to use language – to read, to write, to discuss. And where a child cannot use language effectively, school becomes a daily trial by literacy. Indeed, children will often turn to misbehaviour simply *because* their weak language skills mean they can't access the learning. It feels better to hide that embarrassing fact from their peers by becoming the class clown, than to admit to their weakness.

In the early years of their lives, children's concentration spans are very short. As someone once memorably said to me, teaching preschoolers is 'like herding cats'. This is part of the reason why a child-initiated approach to learning makes sense for preschool-aged children – they will tend to focus on something that holds their interest, but find it much harder to focus on something that the adult asks them to do. Gradually, young children learn how to concentrate for longer and longer periods of time, and on a wider range of activities – including some they don't particularly enjoy. Learning how to do this proves much harder for some than for others. This may be because they have a specific behavioural difficulty, or perhaps simply because of a background of poor parenting approaches.

Impulse control

Babies and very young children typically have poor impulse control – they find it hard to think before they say or do something – they are 'emotionally incontinent'. As we grow older we learn to control that initial emotional response, and to replace it with a more rational and considered one instead. In other words, we learn self-discipline. Even as an adult, however, this is often not an easy thing to do when you're faced with a difficult situation or when you're tired and stressed.

A baby or very young child:

✓ Wants his needs met immediately;
✓ Doesn't understand why sometimes this cannot happen;
✓ May use emotional outbursts as a way of communicating what he wants;
✓ May have a tantrum to try and get what she wants;
✓ May shout or lash out when his desires are frustrated;
✓ Is very prone to being affected emotionally by physical issues, such as feeling hungry, being over tired and so on;
✓ Finds it hard to control her impulses, her emotions and sometimes her feelings of anger.

You may know adults who follow a very similar pattern of behaviour! Certainly, you will have noticed how some children in your early years setting or school will:

✓ Snatch toys or resources off someone else without asking;
✓ Call out the answers when you ask a question of the whole group;
✓ Push to the front of the queue;
✓ Throw a tantrum if they don't get what they want;
✓ Shout to try and get what they want.

These are the children who have poor impulse control.

What causes poor impulse control?

As children grow older, most of them learn how to control these impulses through the way that the adults around them deal with any loss of control. Some parents find it hard to teach their children to control their impulses. Those children with poor impulse control tend to have been parented in one of two ways:

> **Over controlling:** These parents 'baby' the child, so that she is never exposed to situations where she is bored, or tired or expected to step up to the mark. Consequently she never learns how to manage her own emotions in more difficult times. These children are typically slow to become independent and to control their own needs. They will often overreact and be oversensitive to small changes or difficulties in the daily routine.
>
> **Under controlling:** These parents let the child take charge and manipulate them. The child uses tantrums or lashes out, because he has found out that this is the way to get what he wants. This child might also have seen his parents using aggression or bullying to get what they want from others. Consequently he tries to use emotional outbursts as a method of controlling others, rather than learning how to 'manage' his anger.

Developing impulse control

A key part of your role when working with young children is to help them learn how to control or refocus their impulses. Learning how to control their immediate impulses is an important aspect of learning to function within our wider society. We cannot simply scream and throw things and lash out if we do not get what we want. Preschools, nurseries and schools are a kind of miniature version of society – a community of people working together for the best interests of all.

A good example of the importance of impulse control within education is the child's ability to sit on the carpet and raise his hand. You might have noticed how some children will always call out at first, and it takes you a long time to break this habit. Similarly, many aspects of learning to write require self-discipline and a willingness to undertake what might seem 'boring' exercises in order to practice the techniques. The child might not really *want* to practise joining up his letters, but unless he can control that urge to get up and do something else his learning will be hampered.

You can help your children develop impulse control by:

- ✓ Playing games and doing activities which rely on taking turns;
- ✓ Talking about why it's important to share;
- ✓ Boosting their empathy by talking about emotions in relation to behaviour – how does it feel when someone snatches a toy off you?;
- ✓ Ignoring any outbursts or tantrums, unless the child is in immediate danger of hurting himself;
- ✓ Structuring your day so that the children do not get too tired, over excited or bored, so that there is less reason for them to lash out or get upset;
- ✓ Gradually increasing the length of time that the children spend on harder, adult-directed exercises, which require greater levels of self discipline;
- ✓ Making sure not to pay attention to misbehaviour, but to focus on good behaviour instead;
- ✓ Breaking the 'habit' of calling out, by ignoring children who shout out answers and only asking those who have their hands raised;
- ✓ Giving very 'angry' children an outlet for their frustrations – for instance a cushion in a soft area to go and hit if they want to lash out.

As a teacher or practitioner working with young children, you will also need to control your *own* impulses in order to better manage behaviour. This can be tricky because working with young children can be stressful, noisy, messy, hard work. The impulses you need to control might include the impulse to:

- ✓ Snap at children when they don't do what you want, or when they are misbehaving;
- ✓ Raise your voice or shout at the class when you're feeling tired or stressed;
- ✓ Focus far more of your attention on the 'difficult' children than on the 'easy' ones;

✓ Pay attention to misbehaviour, rather than highlighting examples of the behaviour you want. This is much harder to do than it sounds – see the example below.

When dealing with problem behaviour, a good rule of thumb is that you usually don't need to make an immediate intervention unless someone is likely to get hurt, or is hurting others.

Impulse control – for example . . .

I was sitting with some preschool-aged children and some practitioners as a whole group for snack time. There was one adult sitting with each table. Most of the children were waiting very patiently for the snacks to be brought to the tables. However, one child got up from the table and began to crawl around on the floor. My first instinct was to draw attention to the problem by asking him to come back to the table. However, I managed to ignore that impulse, and instead I started chatting to the other children who were sitting on my table, and praising their behaviour. I could see a couple of the other practitioners were itching to intervene, but we all managed to ignore what the child was doing (by now he was rolling around on the floor). Eventually, once he realized that the adults simply weren't interested, he gave up and returned to sit at the table.

Talking about choices

Young children often find it hard to make sensible decisions and good choices, and to understand that they can't always have exactly what they want. When we're very young, we don't know much about how the world works, or about what is good for us. This might be about their day-to-day routines ('Why *can't* I wear my princess dress when it's snowing?'; 'Why *can't* I eat chocolate for dinner every day?') or about their behaviour ('Why *should* I have to sit on the carpet if I don't want to?') Again, this is all tied up with learning impulse control.

As a practitioner, you can use simple choices to help children learn how to make good decisions. As they get older, and understand more about their world, these choices can become more complicated. Being able to make good decisions about what works and what doesn't is important for learning how to manage our behaviour, but also for learning how to create an effective piece of writing.

Your choices might be very simple ones, for instance about your daily routine: *'Do you want milk or water?'*

Or they could be choices used to manage behaviour: *'You have a choice. You can play nicely with this toy instead of banging it on the floor. Or, I can take the toy away and you can go to sit on our thinking spot for a few minutes.'*

Behaviour, listening and noise

Individual writing works best when it is done in a silent, or near silent, working atmosphere, simply because it is easiest to concentrate and to hear your inner 'writing voice'. Some people enjoy music in the background when they write, but others find it very distracting. You (and your children) need to learn how to control the overall noise levels within the classroom or setting as a whole. This can prove tricky, particularly where there are a lot of child-initiated, continuous provision type activities going on. However, once children start at school, the best individual writing will take place in a completely silent classroom.

Some practitioners find it hard to believe that it is possible for very young children to fall completely silent, and to stay that way. I was challenged to demonstrate this the other day with some preschool-aged children. And I was able to get a large group of 2-, 3- and 4-year-olds to fall completely silent for a couple of minutes. Much is to do with the clarity of your expectation, how you present the challenge and the confidence you project when you tell the group this is what they are going to do. Consider the difference between:

> ✗ 'Come on children, could we have a bit of quiet, ssh, ssh, ssh. . . . Look, please can you be quiet, you're really giving me a headache.'

And a clearer, more confident approach:

> ✓ 'Right! [claps hands] Let's see everyone looking this way. Now, when I say "go", I'm going to challenge you to be completely silent for a whole 2 minutes. Do you think you can manage that? Of course you can! Three, two, one . . . go!'

Of course, you need to build up the length of time that the children are asked to be silent, starting small (2 or 3 minutes) and gradually building up the challenge.

Rules about listening and noise

Think carefully about the rules or code of conduct that you use around speaking and listening. Consider the messages that you are sending to the children. If your rule is 'We speak quietly', does this always apply? Are there situations or times (outdoors, during singing, in Physical Education (PE)) that the rule is not really appropriate? At our preschool, we chose '*We use our inside voices inside*' to help the children learn about situation-appropriate behaviour.

With a large group or whole class, it works well to ask the children to practise speaking at different volume levels. By controlling their own sound levels, the children become more conscious about how loud they are speaking, and how well they are listening. You could use 'silent zone' for when we are listening to someone else talking, 'paired voice' for conversations between friends, 'activity voice' for a physical activity and 'outdoor voice' for the louder outdoor environment. Aim to:

> ✓ Use plenty of repetition to ensure that your golden rules are understood;
> ✓ Practice following the rules, for instance getting the class to talk at 'paired voice' level, then at 'activity voice' level;
> ✓ Model the rules at all times for your children;
> ✓ Use non-verbal cues and pauses to encourage better listening, rather than asking for quiet;
> ✓ Create visual representations of your rules so that the children can refer to them;
> ✓ Have a 'focus of the day' or 'focus of the week', rather than trying to get the children to retain a number of rules at once.

Too much noise?

If you frequently find that your setting or classroom gets too loud and it feels like the children are not very good at listening to each other, consider whether your room/activity set-up is contributing to the problem. Constant noise can be very stressful for young children, and indeed for the adults as well. The questions below should help guide your thinking:

- Is there one area of the room where most of the noise happens?
- What kind of activities tend to lead to lots of noise?
- Am I achieving a good balance of activities in the room – some loud, others quieter?
- Do the adults model good listening and reasonable noise levels?
- Are the children getting regular reminders to control the overall noise?
- Are these reminders visual (a noise graph on the board) as well as verbal?
- Is there a gender divide when it comes to noise – is one group (boys/girls) louder than the other?
- If yes, why is this? Do we appear to have different expectations of the children's behaviour and noise levels, depending on whether they are boys or girls?
- Are there places where the children can go to have some quiet time?
- Are there times during the day when the whole class gets some quiet time?

It works well to make a visual representation of how noisy the group is as a whole, to encourage the children to control the overall noise levels by themselves. For instance:

- ✓ A 'noise-o-meter' with a moveable dial – basically a box with a dial fixed on it. Ask your children what level the noise-o-meter should be set at for each activity;
- ✓ A 'noise levels graph' drawn on your board;
- ✓ A 'traffic lights' noise meter, downloaded onto your interactive whiteboard;

✓ You can also buy sets of traffic lights that change colour according to how loud the overall noise levels within the room are getting. See the companion website for more details of where you can buy this resource.

Consider using a variety of sounds and other signals to get the children's attention, particularly when they are doing child-initiated learning and the overall noise levels are high. For instance you might use a bell, a raised hand, a series of claps or a 'join in with me' activity such as Simon Says.

Learning to hold my focus

Writing requires focus – the ability to concentrate on one activity for an extended period of time. Yes, I can scrawl a quick doodle, but if I want to sit and write something meaningful I need to learn how to focus and concentrate. Learning and education in general also require focus. If we hope to learn anything during our schooling, we need to be able to concentrate and pay attention to it. Those children who learn to focus well will do far better in their education. Luckily, concentration and focus are skills that we can help children develop.

You might have noticed that some of your children already have high levels of focus and concentration when they join you from the home environment, while others barely seem able to sustain attention on one thing for more than a few seconds. Some will sit enchanted by a single object or activity, spending many minutes playing with it or studying it. Others will flit from activity to activity, or play with a toy for only moments before discarding it. Those who lack the ability to pay attention will really struggle when they move into the more formal years of schooling. Their 'attention deficit' does not match well with how the curriculum is organized or how learning happens. Not least, the requirement to 'stay in your seat' can be a real struggle for children with poor focus.

There are a number of reasons why some of your children might struggle to focus and pay attention, or to stay still in one place:

✓ An excessive amount of 'screen time' (television, computer games) at an early age;

✓ A lack of stimulation – limited exposure to experiences outside the home, or to high quality toys and undivided adult attention;
✓ Over stimulation – being in an environment which is excessively noisy, or hectic or full of distractions;
✓ A particularly kinaesthetic learning style – they really prefer to get 'hands on' with activities and struggle with static tasks;
✓ A specific special educational need, such as attention deficit hyperactivity disorder (ADHD).

Keep an eye out for those children who really struggle to maintain their focus, or to make eye contact with other children and with adults. If you notice a child who constantly 'flits' from activity to activity, and who finds it very difficult to sit still, flag up your concerns early on. These children often get into trouble with their behaviour almost immediately upon entering a more formal classroom environment. This is especially so when they move from a nursery or preschool environment with a high ratio of adults to children (we use a ratio of about 1 to 5) to a Reception class where there may be one teacher to 30 children.

A really useful rule of thumb for children's concentration spans is their age, plus two. So, when working with young children, you only really have about 5 to 10 minutes in which they will concentrate on a single activity with full focus. That 'single activity' might be you reading them a story, it could be them focusing on circle time or show and tell or it might be them doing a free choice activity. What you'll notice is that, where they have chosen the activity themselves your children will typically be able to focus on it for longer than on an adult-directed task. Of course this rule of thumb doesn't apply to every child equally, nor to every task.

Using focus activities

Help your children develop their focus by doing activities specifically designed to build concentration – activities where they must focus on one thing for an extended period of time. These might be small or large group adult-directed activities during a longer session, or they could be done in a daily circle or registration time where all the children sit together. Here are some suggestions for simple, enjoyable activities:

- Ask the children to close their eyes and focus on listening. What can they hear around them? Can they hear anything outside the room? Encourage them to sit with their eyes closed, simply listening, for gradually extended periods of time. This is a form of meditation, which is particularly relaxing for the children.
- Repeat the listening exercise, but this time instead of asking the children to listen for sounds, encourage them to visualize a story in their heads. You can 'tell' a story ('you are in the woods, look around you, you notice a tower, you walk towards it'). Alternatively, you can encourage the children to visualize a positive image of their own ('you are somewhere warm and comfy, look around and see where you are, what can you see, hear, touch?').
- Get the children to stand in an open space, such as a hall or playground. Explain that you are going to play 'Walk and Freeze'. The children should walk freely around the room, without banging into each other. When they hear you bang a drum, they should freeze completely still. When they hear you bang the drum again, they can start walking again. Repeat several times, until everyone can stop and start at the same moment.
- Ask the children to sit or stand opposite a partner, to do a paired focus activity. Ask them to imagine they are looking in a mirror. When one child moves, the other child should mirror their movements exactly. You might like to demonstrate first, using a mirror, to show them how the opposite hand appears to move when we look at a reflection.
- Do a circle ball throw with your group or class. Stand the whole group in a circle. Explain that you are going to throw a large ball across the circle. You will make eye contact with the child before you throw the ball, so that they know it is coming to them. Each time they are about to throw the ball, the child should make eye contact first.
- 'Statues' is a great favourite of mine for calming a group down, and for encouraging focus. Ask the children to get into a comfy position. Explain that, when you say 'go', they are going to freeze as still as statues. They must keep their hands, feet and eyes still, although they are allowed to breathe. At first, you may find that younger children struggle to stay still at all. However,

if you build up the time gradually they learn how to focus on holding their bodies still. You might also know this activity as 'sleeping lions'.

Mucky focus: learning to become absorbed

The ability to become absorbed in something, to the exclusion of all else, is something that you might have noticed in even the youngest of children. In fact, often young children are *more* able than adults to fall into a focus – whether in an imaginative world, or a purely earthbound one. This is sometimes termed a 'working meditation' – the kind of 'in the zone' mental state you achieve when you're doing something that you really enjoy. Hours pass while seeming like minutes. I find it easiest to achieve this mental state when I'm gardening and (of course) when I'm writing.

This absorption and focus is essential for learning to write, and for sticking at writing when you're doing it. Where it tends to happen in the early years is when the child is involved in a particularly mucky, and multisensory, experience. The fact that all or most of the senses are involved really seems to 'hook' a child into an activity. There's the added bonus that sensory play is often great for fine motor control. It's also great for learning to really feel objects through your fingers, and consequently to be more able to feel and manipulate a writing tool. Mucky play happens most easily in the great outdoors, using natural materials.

I can well remember my own son being fascinated by mud when he was tiny, and spending hours out in the garden pouring water onto soil and getting his toy diggers 'stuck' in it. We built on this interest together, moving different materials around with the diggers, and getting really engrossed in the garden. Throughout all of this, he was learning how to focus, how to use his hands and fingers and also how the world around him works.

Recently, I watched one of our preschoolers completely engrossed in scooping out the squishy insides of a pumpkin, to make a Halloween lantern. From time to time, she would extract a small piece of pumpkin, hold it to her nose, sniff it, frown a bit, give it a little lick and then put it to one side. The focus and concentration in what she was doing was extraordinary. (See the 'Practical Project' and the photo below for more on this pumpkin activity.)

'Mucky' activities

When you offer 'mucky' or 'messy' activities, you might set up some which are just for child-initiated exploration (playing with water and soil), and others with more of a specific purpose (finding bugs that are hidden in the ground and counting them). Some parents can be resistant to the idea of their children getting covered in gloop or mud. If this is the case at your setting you might:

✔ Have a dedicated 'mucky day' and ask parents to send in their children in old clothes;
✔ Put regular reminders in a parent newsletter, explaining how important messy play is, and how it will take place regularly at your setting;
✔ Buy a set of waterproof, washable, outdoor overalls for the children to wear;
✔ Run a 'mucky play' workshop, to help parents understand how valuable this kind of exploration is.

Use the following list of 'mucky' activities to get your children absorbed and learning how to focus. These activities are all great for fine motor skills as well:

✔ Make some corn flour 'gloop' – slowly add one cup of cold water to two cups of corn flour in a bowl. This makes a lovely, sensory kind of 'gloop' mixture for the children to feel and play with.
✔ If/when it snows, gather some snow to take indoors, so that the children can get 'hands on' with it.
✔ Make 'creepy crawly jelly' – set some plastic insects in jelly, for the children to dig out.
✔ Fill a plastic book tray with water and some objects around a theme – different leaves and natural materials work well. Freeze the tray overnight in your freezer. Now put this out in your water tray or tuff tray, so that the children can experiment with how ice feels and how it melts. The children love waiting for the objects to be 'released' from the block.
✔ Put a load of cooked spaghetti in your water tray for the children to handle. Offer tools such as chopsticks for them to use to pick up the strands. Add a little bit of washing up liquid to keep the pasta slippery.

✓ Make up a load of porridge for mucky play around a 'Goldilocks and the Three Bears' theme.

✓ Mix up a load of Gelli Baff for your water tray, putting different toys related to a particular 'theme' in it for the children to play with.

✓ Put some soapy water into a tuff spot, along with a plastic hula hoop. Get your children to stand in the middle, then slowly pull up the hoop. With luck they will be standing in a giant bubble!

✓ Create some papier mâché masks, using newspaper and glue. First, blow up a balloon and then cover this with torn up strips of newspaper soaked in glue, in layers. Do this over several days and then leave to dry thoroughly. Cut the balloon in half to make two mask shapes, then cut holes for the eyes and mouth, decorate and add some elastic.

*   *   *

Practical project – Pumpkin party

Note: This activity can be done with bought pumpkins, or you can grow your own!

You will need

Grow your own version

- A large piece of open ground suitable for growing (we are lucky enough to have access to an allotment);
- Giant pumpkin seeds ('American Giant' seeds work well for a really giant pumpkin);
- A greenhouse to get your seeds started;
- Pots, compost, trowels;
- Large pieces of cardboard;
- Several large pumpkins;
- Several spoons;
- A sharp knife (for adult use only);
- Marker pens;
- A1 sheets of paper;
- Orange paint and paint brushes.

Learning intentions

- To develop fine motor skills (planting seeds, scooping out the pumpkin flesh);
- To explore all the senses;

- To develop focus and concentration;
- To practise mark making skills;
- And, for the grow-your-own version, to learn patience, how plants grow and about the seasons.

Instructions

This is a great activity for Harvest Festival and Halloween time. You will need to think well ahead if you are doing the 'grow-your-own version'. (NB: The 'grow-your-own' version works best if the same children grow the pumpkins and make the lanterns, so is most suitable for a nursery or preschool where the children stay for more than one academic year.)

To grow your own: Get the children to plant their seeds in small pots, a couple of centimetres deep. If you have access to a greenhouse, you can do this in about April. Alternatively, plant your seeds outdoors after all danger of frost has passed. Pumpkins grow best when planted into very rich soil – if you have access to well rotted manure or a compost heap, they will happily grow directly in this. They are very self-sufficient and will spread quickly to cover the ground. To give them some extra care and to ensure a really beautiful crop, put pieces of cardboard under the pumpkin fruits as they form.

To have a pumpkin party: Take your children to harvest their pumpkins in late October. If you've grown 'American Giant' you will need a wheelbarrow or trolley to move them. Alternatively, buy several pumpkins from the supermarket just before Halloween.

Offer the children some A1 size sheets of paper to 'design' a face for their pumpkins using shapes such as triangles for the eyes and mouth. You might like to give them a template of a pumpkin shape, or let them draw this themselves. Use marker pens and orange paint to finish your designs.

Now make a slit in the top of the pumpkin with a sharp knife and let the children lift off the lid. Finally use the spoons to scoop the flesh out from the pumpkins and carve the face for the children. And to complete the cycle you can of course use the pumpkin flesh for some cooking, and the seeds for next year's crop.

* * *

In the photos below, you can see the children involved in our pumpkin lantern making activity. The first photo shows Niamh planning and painting her design. The second photo shows the children scooping out the insides of the pumpkin with spoons – this is fantastic for both sensory exploration and also for building hand and finger strength.

In this section . . .

- Explore how children convey meaning through their marks
- Help your children acquire the concepts needed for writing
- Examine how children learn to write their names
- Explore the role of shapes and symbols within writing
- Learn how stories enhance your children's conceptual development
- Find fascinating ways to use non-fiction texts in your setting

Consider this . . .

Letters and words are basically a series of shapes and symbols. In most languages these shapes correlate to the sounds we make within our speech. We can 'sound out' the letters of a word to read it, or to write it and gain meaning from it or to use it to convey meaning to others. A key developmental step for young children is to understand that these different shapes, and combinations of shapes, equate to different letters, phonemes and therefore sounds within the English language. Of course, this is a key step in learning to read – by blending together individual letter sounds and phonemes the child learns to make sense of what different words say. (Although remember that English is not a regular language – there are a number of words where sounding out alone is not enough – see Signpost 8 for much more on this.)

Sharing stories is perhaps the most important and regular way in which we show young children that marks on a page hold both sound and meaning. If a child is read to every day from a very young age, this reinforces the notion that books and print are an important part of our culture and our society. The child also starts to learn that books work in a particular way – they are (in English) read from front to back, from the left-hand side of the page to the right-hand side and from the top of the page to the bottom. When the child himself comes to read and write stories, he will mirror the 'book behaviours' that he has learned in the early years from his parents or carers, and from you.

Of course, as well as understanding that marks made by someone else hold meaning, children also begin to express their own patterns of thought through the marks that they make. Before they are able to form the actual letters, you will see them making meaning through the marks and symbols that they use. Look closely at a child's pictures and marks and you can gain a sense of how they see the world, and what kind of meanings they ascribe to it.

Mark making and schemas

Mark making can help young children make sense of their world, and express to others how they see the world. The patterns of marks that you observe in young children can help you understand their patterns of thought, even before they can express what they actually 'mean'. You may be used to observing children's 'schemas': those regular patterns of play identified by Piaget, which help the child organize their knowledge and relate to the world. For instance:

- ✓ A transportation schema – a child who enjoys moving blocks and toys from one place to another, and who loves filling up bags;
- ✓ An enclosure schema – a child who often fills up containers, or who loves to climb inside boxes;
- ✓ A transforming schema – a child who loves to turn one thing into something else, for instance adding paint to the sand.

Often, these patterns of thought also come out in young children's mark making. For instance some children become particularly fascinated by a specific object/animal – every mark becomes a representation of that thing. In the photo below you can see Shay using mark making to express his fascination with sharks (he has been enjoying the film *Finding Nemo*).

Similarly, young children's earliest mark making will often feature images of people. In the piece below, done by a 3-year-old child, you can see definite signs of faces, and perhaps some shapes meant to denote letters as well. Clearly, children are trying to make meaning with their writing, right from the earliest chance they have.

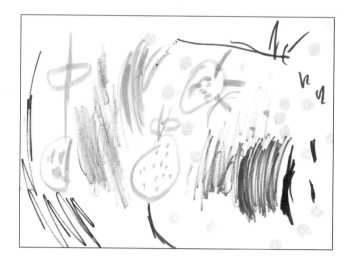

Signs and symbols

We are surrounded by signs and symbols – their power to convey a simple meaning quickly and forcefully is clearly understood by advertisers and marketers. Well before they can read words, children will understand what many of these symbols mean. Just try showing your children the golden 'M' symbol used by McDonalds, or the tick used by Nike. You may be surprised at how many of your children can instantly tell you what these symbols mean.

The visual nature of a symbol means that it is easily understood, even by young children, and this makes symbols and graphic pictures very useful for conveying meaning within your setting. The meaning of a symbol is put across via shape and colour, as well as through any writing that it includes. In your setting, you can use symbols and signs to help the children understand routines and structures, and also to learn about communicating meaning through marks. Symbols are also very useful for children who have English as an additional language. You could use symbols to create:

- ✓ A visual register, using various signs and symbols. For instance the children could put their name on the 'sad' or 'happy' side of a board, or under a picture of the drink they would like at snack time.
- ✓ Visual timetables, for the whole group or for individuals, with images showing what happens at different times of the day.
- ✓ Labels within areas in your setting, for instance a 'Germ Busters' sign in the toilets.
- ✓ Symbols for each of your golden rules, to back up discussions about what the rules mean.
- ✓ Stickers with symbols on them, to give to children as a reward.
- ✓ Signs written in different community languages.

*   *   *

Practical project – Stop, go, no entry!

You will need

- ✓ Poles or mop/broom handles;
- ✓ Large pieces of cardboard;
- ✓ A pair of scissors;
- ✓ Paints or felt tip pens;
- ✓ Gaffer tape or heavy duty parcel tape;
- ✓ Ride on toys;
- ✓ Outdoor chalks.

Learning intentions

  ✓ To examine how different shapes and symbols have different meanings;
  ✓ To use these symbols within an imaginative context;
  ✓ To mark make on different surfaces.

Instructions

Although you can buy plenty of ready-made 'road signs', it's far more fun and educationally valuable to get your children to make some of their own. You might choose No Entry (a red circle with a white line across), Stop (a red octagon with STOP written in white), Mini Roundabout (a blue circle with three arrows going round) or perhaps some speed limits (written with black numbers on a white circle, with a red line around it).

Show the children a variety of signs and symbols, and talk about what these mean. Discuss the different colours that are used – why do they think red is chosen for signs that give an order or a limit? You might also go for a walk around your local area, perhaps using a digital camera, so that the children can take photos of different signs. Now explain that you are going to create a road system for the ride on toys, with signs to show directions, speed limits and so on.

Create your signs by painting the cardboard shapes and then attaching them to the poles. Get the children to draw a series of roads on the ground, using outdoor chalks. They can then experiment with 'driving' their cars and other vehicles around the roads, following the instructions on the signs.

Visit the companion website for a link to the Direct Gov site, which offers downloadable PDFs of different types of road signs.

*   *   *

Me and my name

Our names are a crucial part of who we are – they give us a sense of identity, attachment and belonging. Right from the earliest moments of our lives we hear our names over and over, most often being spoken by the people that we love. Using marks to write their own name is one of the first pieces of writing that many children will try to do – saying, in effect, 'this is me'! Just think of the graffiti that has existed from ancient times – the urge to mark our name on public surfaces is a very strong one indeed.

There are plenty of ways you can motivate your children to learn the shape and letters of their name, and to make marks to write it:

- ✓ Get your children to self-register using their name – at pre-school we use name labels with Velcro on the back kept in a tray. Parents are encouraged to help their children find their own name and stick it onto the registration board. By seeing and picking out their names every day, the children become used to seeing the shape and identifying it as 'theirs'.
- ✓ Put children's names on their pegs and book trays. Include a picture beside the name, which remains consistent every time the child's name is used. You can link the initial sound of the image to the child's name, for instance a 'Train' for 'Tommy', to help him learn that first sound/letter in his name.
- ✓ As the children get older, and start to recognize their names, remove the picture from beside the name so that they identify the actual word.
- ✓ Later on, encourage them to replace the adult written name tags with ones they have written themselves.
- ✓ When children draw or paint a picture, or make a model, encourage them to participate in 'writing their name' on it.
- ✓ Write name labels in other situations – for instance when planting and growing sunflowers.
- ✓ Offer the children a laminated copy of their name, with arrows to show them which way to write. We offer opportunities for our older or more able children to practise tracing over their name. It's important to have close adult supervision when they do this, to ensure that they are forming the letters correctly.

You can also use art based, creative approaches to encourage the children to become familiar with their names. They could:

- ✓ Make their name out of twigs;
- ✓ Shape and bake the letters of their name using dough;
- ✓ Ice cakes with the initial letter of their name;

✓ Use magazine cut outs/collage techniques to make their name;

✓ Write their names using silver or gold pens, on black paper.

Dealing with parent pressure to write names

Parents are often especially keen to see their children writing their names – it seems to them the logical first step in 'learning how to write'. At our setting, we've found that there's quite a bit of pressure from some parents for us to sit their children down in a formal way, and get them to trace over their names regularly until they learn to write them. We've also had some children who have been 'taught' to write their names at home, through repeated practice (and sometimes even in capital letters). Of course, there's no reason why parents should know how early writing develops. Equally, some parents will have gone to school at a time when teaching was done in a far more formal way. So, it's important and useful to communicate information to parents about this part of early child development. You might:

✓ Use leaflets, parent workshops and 'hands on' sessions to explain about the best approaches to develop early mark making.

✓ Help parents understand that it is typically counter productive to get very young children to write their names 'properly'. If children do not have the finger strength to form the letters correctly, they can very quickly get into bad habits around letter formation or pencil grip. These habits then have to be broken later on.

✓ Similarly, be clear that it can be off putting for young children to see 'writing my name' as an enforced task, and consequently demotivate them from wanting to write.

✓ For older children, who have developed sufficient pre-writing skills, offer concerned parents a laminated guide showing how the child should form the letters of his or her name correctly.

Interestingly, children come to writing their name at different times, but it is very rare indeed (even for children with special needs) that they never learn to write it at all. It's the classic reassurance when you're toilet training your children – they won't still be in nappies when aged 15! In the picture below you can see how the process develops over the course of several years:

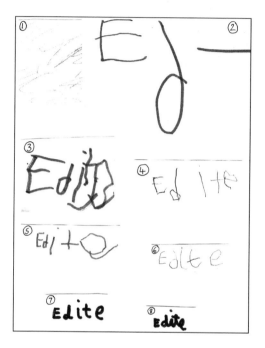

1. First marks made at age 2 – a sample from a postcard written by Edite which she told us said 'Edite is going to Portugal'.
2. Age 3, we can start to see the first clear letter shapes beginning to emerge.
3. Age 3 and a half, Edite's name is starting to become more recognizable.
4. Age 4, in the term before starting school, the writing is wobbly but easy to read – she had been practising tracing over her name.
5. and 6. Age 4 and 5 in Reception – notice how the letter 'e' is hard for her to write at first, but by the end of the year all the letters are correctly formed.
7. and 8. Age 5 and rising 6 in Year 1 – Edite can now print neatly, and has just learned cursive writing, so is keen to practise joining her name up.

And here is a photo of Edite focusing closely on writing her name, a couple of weeks before she turned 6.

*   *   *

 Practical project – Graffiti wall

WARNING: Only for the brave!

You will need

✓ A flat area of wall in your outdoor area;
✓ Alternatively, an outdoor chalkboard, or chalkboard paint;
✓ Outdoor chalks;
✓ Paint or large marker pens (if you're allowed a permanent wall).

Learning intentions

✓ To encourage children to mark make their names;
✓ To see writing as an act of public expression.

Instructions

There's something peculiarly enthralling for children about writing on a wall (particularly where that writing is permanent). You might get them to mark make directly onto a brick wall. Alternatively, you could fix up a chalkboard, or paint a section of wall, fence or the side of a shed with chalkboard paint.

If you have an understanding head teacher or setting leader, why not suggest the idea of a permanent 'graffiti wall' for the children? This is simply a wall that is designated for public art/writing using permanent writing tools. It can be painted over several times a year, as it gets full of marks. Your 'graffiti wall' could be a section of wall indoors, or an area outside.

Parents may well worry that you are giving the children free rein to write on the walls at home. However, what you are actually doing is teaching situation appropriate behaviour. Make it clear to the children that it is *only* this section of wall on which they can make their marks. For older children with a better grasp of written language, set rules about the kind of language they can use, and also about not making personal comments about other children.

If you're nervous with this idea, you can always cover a section of wall, or the top of a table, with lining paper. Or you could buy some wooden tables and chairs for the children to decorate – it's essentially the same thing.

*   *   *

'Graffiti mark making' – for example . . .

My daughter showed a strong urge to mark make on her bedroom walls, from about 3 years of age. At first we resisted the idea, and tried to wipe the marks off and stop her doing it. But after a while it occurred to us that this was actually proving a really positive activity in terms of her mark making. So, we made it clear that it was only her bedroom walls where this was allowed. Her walls now chart a fascinating journey from first marks, to letters, to words, to the names of her friends, and now to whole sentences. And she has never shown any inclination to write on any other walls in the house.

Seeing shapes

a b c d e f g h i j k l m n o p q r s t u v w x y z

If you stop for a moment and look at the alphabet as it's written above, you will start to notice that each letter is made up of a distinctive set of shapes. There are circles and part circles, in the letters 'a', 'b', 'c' and 'o', among others. There are vertical lines, for instance in the letters 'b', 'l' and 't'. There are horizontal lines, for example in 'f' and in 'z', and horizontal curves in the letter 's'. And of course there are a couple of dots, some diagonal lines and plenty of mountainous bumps as well.

Children need to learn and practice these different movements because they need to be able physically to write them, and also to get them ingrained in their physical memories. They also need to learn to see the 'shape' of a word as an essential aspect of learning to read (it's not *all* about phonics.) At first, children should make these shapes on a large scale, using movements right from the shoulder. As they get older, and gain more control, the shape movements will become smaller and smaller until they can make the very fine movements needed to hold and control a pencil.

There are a number of key gross and fine motor movements for your children to develop to support their handwriting. These are:

- ✓ Vertical Arcs – swiping in an up and down movement;
- ✓ Horizontal Arcs – fanning and wiping from side to side;
- ✓ Diagonal Arcs – swiping from side to side, on an angle, in both directions;
- ✓ Push/Pull/Press – large reaching, grasping and pressing movements;
- ✓ Circles – moving around in a circular, anticlockwise motion.

Note: The anticlockwise motion is important because of the way letters are written.

These movements simulate the shapes that need to be learned to write letters. For instance the vertical arc of a lowercase letter 't' or 'l', the sideways snaking motion of a letter 's' and the push to dot a letter 'i'. Get your children to practise these movements on a large scale (with the whole arm), and also gradually on a smaller scale (with the fingers, with a writing tool). The point at which children are ready to make smaller scale shapes will vary hugely. In the photo you can see Matty, who has only just had his third birthday.

As you can see from the photo, Matty is already able to make accurate anticlockwise circles on a whiteboard. His gross and fine motor control, and pen grip, is unusually well developed for a young child. This activity was self-initiated rather than adult-directed – Matty enjoys taking part in mark making and is happy to focus on it for extended periods of time.

Active writing movements

Boys love the idea of martial arts movements – so get them doing some 'Kung Fu' writing to practise their writing movements (this idea is inspired by Phil Beadle's 'Kung Fu Punctuation' for older writers). Practise the movements and strokes given above, introducing them as 'Kung Fu' style movements for your superhero writers to complete. (In a similar vein, you can 'dance' the strokes alongside stories, songs or rhymes, using the 'Write Dance' materials – published by Lucky Duck, 2010.)

Your children could:

- ✓ Write giant letter shapes in the air ('sky writing');
- ✓ Write letter shapes on each other's backs;
- ✓ Move ribbons through the air to create different shapes;
- ✓ Paint shapes in 'magic water' (water with glitter in it);
- ✓ 'Draw' shapes with a torch in a darkened tent;
- ✓ Make shadow shapes with their fingers;
- ✓ Write with a 'magic wand', created out of a kitchen roll tube and crepe paper (or a light sabre for any *Star Wars* mad children);
- ✓ Trace around shapes and mazes that you've drawn on a sheet of paper;
- ✓ Walk around shapes and strokes that you have taped out on the floor.

Drawing these strokes in tactile materials works particularly well in encouraging children to feel confident about making different strokes and shapes. It also helps the children to assimilate these strokes fully into their physical memory. For instance they might:

- ✓ Make large-scale patterns in mud or paint with their fingers or their toes;
- ✓ Draw different shapes and strokes in shaving foam, or in whipped cream;
- ✓ Carve shapes in sand using twigs;
- ✓ Make lines and shapes in a piece of clay or play dough.

If you're lucky enough to have access to a beach near your setting, there can hardly be any tactile material better than wet sand for practising writing strokes and making shapes with a finger or a stick.

When your children are involved in mark making activities, use vocabulary to describe the kind of movements and shapes that they are making, and encourage them to do the same. For instance you might talk about how '*I love the way you're sweeping the paint round in circles*', or '*Those lines you've done are really jagged, aren't they?*'

*   *   *

 ## Practical project – Shape walk

You will need

- An outdoor space or a planned walk somewhere local;
- A digital camera;

- A clipboard and a pen;
- A bag in which to collect any natural shapes you find.

Learning intentions

- To get the children talking about shapes and using their names;
- To explore how shapes can communicate meaning;
- To encourage the children to use their thinking and questioning skills.

Instructions

Take your children on a 'shape walk' – a walk around your local environment during which you 'collect' as many shapes as you can. You might collect a specific item to take back to your setting (a round conker, a spiky leaf) or you could take a photo of a shaped item that cannot be moved (a triangular road sign, a square building). Encourage the children to identify any shapes that have particular meanings. For instance a zebra crossing where the different coloured rectangles indicate that it is safe to cross, and the zigzag lines indicating that no one should park close by.

When you return to your setting, you could sort the shapes into different types, you could trace around or over them or you could make some shape collages using a variety of natural materials. All the while, of course, talking about the names of the shapes and the kind of movements needed to make them.

* * *

Using stories

Stories have the potential to support your children's conceptual development, and their pre-writing and writing skills, in a whole host of different ways. Hearing plenty of stories, and looking at plenty of books, will of course help your children understand the basic concept of this chapter: that marks on the page hold meaning. And in time, they can use those same marks to create meanings and stories of their own, through their writing.

Although young children may not yet be able to write a story in the sense that we know it, they will be learning and assimilating vital information about how stories are constructed and created. They will also be learning 'story language' – words such as 'character', 'hero', 'setting' – as well as 'story phrases' – 'once upon a time' and 'in a land far far away'. Interestingly, as well as accessing this information through books, your children will also be learning it through television and film. The popularity of Disney films, superheroes, cartoon characters, all feeds into your children learning about how stories are created.

Information about how stories work will be important in helping them write their own stories as they grow older. The more explicit you can make this information now, the better able they will be to use it later on. When you read a story to your children, help them understand the key features of stories. You can do this through discussion, through the way that you tell the stories and also through asking questions and getting the children to ask questions in return. Help them understand that:

> ✓ Stories have a beginning, a middle and an end;
> ✓ Stories have a sequence – this event, followed by that event, finishing up with this event;
> ✓ Stories use a particular kind of story language – openers such as 'Once upon a time' and repeated phrases such as 'run, run, as fast as you can';
> ✓ For school-aged children, talk about how sequences are shown through the use of connectives (joining words);
> ✓ There are different kinds of 'stock' characters within a story – some good (heroes, heroines), some not so good (villains, 'baddies');
> ✓ Many stories have a happy ending, particularly fairy tales.

Depending on the age of your children, you can introduce different levels of story vocabulary – early on, children might be familiar with words such as 'baddies', while later on this becomes 'villains'. Similarly, words such as 'genre' and 'narrative' can be introduced to school-aged children. In my experience, I've found that children love to learn technical sounding terms that you might think are a bit complicated for them to understand.

Creating story maps

Story maps are an excellent way to help children understand more about how stories are structured. The basic idea of a story map is that you take a series of events from a story, and then map them out in a visual way. The teacher or practitioner gets the children to identify the sequence of events, and these are then transformed by the children and/or the teacher into a visual representation of the story. While you're creating a story map, you can start introducing connectives/conjunctions to the class – words such as 'next', 'then', 'so' and 'after that'.

Your visual representation might be:

- ✓ On a sheet of A1 size paper, or on a length of lining paper;
- ✓ Using pegs to peg up pictures of the events in sequence on a washing line;
- ✓ On a storyboard sheet, using photos of each story event as 'stills';
- ✓ Using a set of photocopied pictures, asking the children to work out what order the events appear in the story.

Stories and conceptual development

Of course, stories can do a whole lot more for young children than simply show them the link between books and writing. The subtle nature of language, and of stories, means that it can introduce a child to layers of understanding far beyond that which they might be able to articulate at this age. The power of stories to support the concepts, as explained below, makes a very strong case for their frequent use within every early years setting.

Developing imagination

Stories require us to use our imagination – to create a mental picture of something that isn't real. Where the storyteller uses a picture book, the child is helped to create a mental picture by looking at the images. But most young children are capable of creating this mental picture without even having to see the images. Indeed, if you usually always tell stories using a book, you should practise retelling some well-known stories simply with words. It's the words that create the images in the children's heads, as much as it is the pictures. Listening out for the words, and pulling out meaning from them, is a vital skill for children to learn as they move into their school years.

Entering the fiction

The understanding that some things are real, while others are made up, is a key stage in children's conceptual development. Young children are very willing to 'enter the fiction' of a story, for instance by playing doctors and nurses in your role play area. They use this to experiment with how they might behave in different situations, as well as enjoying the chance to play at being someone else. Young children find it easy to 'suspend their disbelief' (typically, much easier than adults do). A young child will happily talk to a toy baby as though it is real – an adult might feel embarrassed to do the same. By entering lots of different fictional worlds, young children start to make sense of themselves and their place within society. They also start to experiment with symbolism – the twig 'stands for' a magic wand in that game of fairies and wizards.

A widening vocabulary

We use a much wider and more varied vocabulary when we read and write, than we do when we speak. So, by being exposed to lots and lots of stories, children are simultaneously exposed to lots and lots of new and interesting words. Children can sound out a word much more easily (see the next chapter) if they know what it is meant to sound like in the first place. In other words, if they have heard a word used frequently, for instance in a story, they are far more likely to be able to sound it out once they gain knowledge about letter sounds and letter blends.

Words and meaning

Stories also allow children to hear new (or already known) words in different contexts. They start to see that the same word (two, too, to) can mean different things in different situations when used within a text. Children learn to extract meaning from the context in which a word is heard, but also through the way that it has been said by the person reading them the story. Although a child can be taught to read a page of text through a system such as synthetic phonics, this has little value unless the child can also grasp the full *meaning* of that text. Hearing lots of stories helps children understand the important of context, subtleties and nuance in gathering meaning.

As well as seeing how different words have different meanings, your children will also be developing their comprehension skills. Ask questions after you've told a story to check for their levels of understanding, and to check that the story was pitched at the right level.

Story structure and elements

Similarly, as they listen to a story children will hear and learn about the use of different tenses, connectives (linking words) and scripted dialogue – all of the features that your children will eventually need to use in their own writing. They start to see that different stories fall within different genres – there are stories full of action, fairy tales, myths, ghost stories and so on. Each genre has its own particular 'language' of elements.

Language and layers of meaning

Listening to stories can allow even a young child to begin to understand that language has layers of meaning within it. Stories expose them to complex higher order concepts, such as symbolism and metaphor (see below for examples). Although very young children wouldn't be able to use these words to say what the language within stories is doing, they can still assimilate the concepts. And hopefully, later on, use these same features in their own writing.

Symbolism: Many children's stories use colour in a symbolic way. In *Little Red Riding Hood*, the cloak is red – the colour of danger, and of blood. Similarly, the wolf symbolizes the dangers that lurk within the forest.

Metaphor: Many fairy stories use a metaphor to show good triumphing over evil. For example, in *Snow White and the Seven Dwarves*, the evil queen is eventually overcome by the prince's love for Snow White. The dwarves represent different human traits, and the mirror on the wall symbolizes the evil queen's vanity.

Playing with words

Stories often invite the reader/listener to engage in word play – they use rhyme, alliteration, tongue twisters, and other linguistic devices based around the sound of words. Learning to listen for alliteration and rhyme are both crucial phases in developing the ability to read, and subsequently to write. Hearing lots of stories will help your children get comfy with listening out for words that sound the same. (See the next chapter for lots more on words and sounds.)

New experiences

Through stories, your children can learn about other lives, other experiences, other cultures, other places, other people or other creatures – both real, and imagined. Through stories, you and your children can travel to the moon, sail around the world, visit a royal palace or ride on a dragon. This access to new experiences is perhaps particularly important for those children who have had a limited range of experiences in their everyday lives.

Similarly, stories can help your children examine experiences they have gone through, or those which they might be facing. You can find stories that deal with many new or difficult situations such as moving house, a visit to the dentist or the loss of someone close. Through hearing how someone else has dealt with those situations, your children can gain confidence and security.

A sense of our place

Stories help us find out about our place in the world, and our place within the history of humanity. Many stories have ancient roots – myths, fables, parables or fairy tales which all go back many hundreds and sometimes even thousands of years. And by telling and retelling these stories to each generation, we link ourselves and our children with the storytellers who came before us. Stories can also help us learn about different cultures, or to find out more about our own culture and our place within it.

Moral codes

Stories often come with a moral code (often hidden within the text, rather than stated explicitly). Stories help us understand what is right, and what is wrong. It's no accident that many key religious texts use stories and parables to define a moral code for their followers. In an increasingly secular world stories can give us a moral framework by which to live.

For instance in *The Snail and the Whale* (by Julia Donaldson and Axel Scheffler, published by MacMillan), the moral is that it doesn't matter how big or small you are, what matters is determination and courage. This is what allows the tiny snail to save the whale when it gets beached in the bay. Some children will access the story on its simplest level, as a lovely tale with gorgeous illustrations. But others will be able to see the message *behind* the text, again a key concept for their future writing.

Stories also help us learn how different people might behave in different situations, and how sometimes they do the right thing, and sometimes they don't. A story can help us see the consequences and outcomes of different kinds of behaviour – both for ourselves, and for others. In this way, they can help your children examine emotions and develop the key skill of empathy.

Problem solving, sequencing and prediction

Stories offer a great opportunity to get your children thinking about how characters approach and solve problems, and consequently how they might do the same. How can I build a house that is wolf proof? How can a tiny snail communicate the message that the whale is in danger? How can the mouse in *The Gruffalo* persuade the monster not to eat him? These challenges add dramatic tension to the story – a crucial element in creating a well-structured piece of fiction.

As they listen to a story, children learn to use prediction – what happens next, what is the cause and effect here, what are the consequences of the characters' actions? After listening to a story, the children might take that story into their role play, for instance recreating elements of a story or reusing the vocabulary they have heard in different situations.

Social interaction

Telling, and listening to, a story is of course a social interaction between people. By sharing a story together we build our relationship together, we begin to bond and we show that we care for each other. And, of course, we should never forget that stories are a huge source of pleasure, both for children and for adults. The very act of telling or listening to a story brings people together in a comfortable, relaxed and happy environment.

Enhancing your reading area

By offering a comfy area for storytelling and story reading, you will help your children associate stories with feeling safe, secure and happy. Their experience at your setting should mirror the experience that they (hopefully) get at home – of reading being a warm, cosy and enjoyable activity. Sharing stories at night, safe, snug and warm in their beds with a loved one next to them creates a powerful feeling of security and happiness. Similarly, sharing stories with you and their peer group in your setting can invoke that same feeling.

A lot of the time teachers and practitioners share stories with a large group or a whole class, with the children relaxing on the carpet as you read. Make your carpet area as comfy as possible – have a selection of cushions or beanbags if you can. If you have washable or wipe clean cushions, these can be used outdoors for reading stories together in the summer months. During child-initiated times in your setting or classroom ensure that the children can make a choice to sit and read or look at books. This might be with a practitioner, but it might also be something that they choose to do with their friends.

To enhance your reading area:

- ✓ Try to screen it off in some way – for instance with a partition, by hanging materials from a net curtain wire to make 'curtains', or by using a tent or tepee.
- ✓ Offer some comfy seating – a child sized sofa or a set of beanbags.
- ✓ Include a selection of books – both fiction and non-fiction. Depending on the amount of space you have these could be displayed in a book shelf, or in a hanging book rack suspended from the wall.

✓ If space allows, keep your reading area away from the noisy activities on offer.

✓ Consider using a 'theme' for your reading area – I once saw a beautiful 'Winnie the Witch' styled reading area in a Reception class which had a black tent, with torches and bats hanging all around.

Different forms of writing

As well as getting the concept that 'marks hold meaning', your children also need to understand that writing comes in many different forms, and how they can use these forms to communicate. In the pre-writing stage these different forms of writing might be incorporated into child initiated play, for instance as 'menus' and 'order pads' in a café role play area. In more adult-directed activities, the children could create and write in Christmas cards for their parents, or write labels to go on a display.

Non-fiction forms

Expose your children to lots of non-fiction forms, both as part of the continuous provision of activities, during the day-to-day routine within your setting, and in the displays you have around the place. Put plenty of labels in your teaching space, using large, bold, lower-case print. Here are some of the key non-fiction forms for early years practitioners and teachers, with some ideas about how you might use them:

✓ Labels (the parts of a flower);

✓ Recipes (to make your mum happy);

✓ Shopping lists (Santa's list of presents to buy for Christmas);

✓ Spell ingredients (for a spell to turn you into a princess);

✓ Postcards (sent home from abroad);

✓ Birthday cards (for their parents or friends);

✓ Invitations (to the Ugly Sisters in Cinderella);

✓ Posters (about good hand washing);

✓ Reports (a school report on a character from a book);

✓ Instructions (how to build a Lego model).

In the image above, you can see a piece of writing done by a child who has just started in Reception. He had shown a particular interest in building with Lego, and used it a great deal at home. He came into school with this set of instructions for building a Lego model. You can see from this writing that he is able to sequence events, and write a clear set of instructions in numbered order, even though he has yet to learn to write using words.

Using frameworks

Frameworks, or writing frames, give children a 'frame' on which to hang their writing. This helps you introduce them to the format of different kinds of non-fiction writing, and also to boost their confidence in creating a similar piece of writing. At the preschool stage, this might simply be a postcard for them to put in your postbox, or a passport style booklet when you're doing an airport theme around the summer holidays. In the Reception class and in Key Stage One, your writing frames can become more complex, and the children can have more involvement in creating them. Even with young children, you can complete a piece of writing as a whole group, with the children giving the ideas and the practitioner filling in the writing frame. When using frames:

✓ Show the children examples of lots of different pieces of writing in this form – for instance a selection of recipe books;
✓ Examine these texts closely and talk together about the elements that are common to this particular form;
✓ Create a 'frame' for your children on your interactive whiteboard, and work together to complete an example;
✓ Brainstorm a set of key vocabulary with the children, or offer key words on small cards for them to copy.

You can differentiate your frames for children of different ability levels by adapting the amount of 'fill in the blanks' required – leaving more gaps for the more able writers. You can also give more support to those children who struggle to find the vocabulary they need.

In the image above, you can see a recipe produced using a writing frame. The 5-year-old Reception class child completed the activity mainly by herself. The task was adult-directed, and the child had a bit of support from the teacher in finding the right vocabulary. Notice how some of the key vocabulary was written on the board for the class; others were words where the child requested the spelling from the teacher.

In this sample, you can see the child making sensible guesses about spellings based on her current levels of phonic knowledge: 'chopt', 'paton' (for pattern), 'ayt' (for ate).

Boys and non-fiction forms

Boys are often particularly attracted to non-fiction forms of writing – they just seem to love finding out about how things work, how they go together and how they are taken apart again. The writing sample below was a self-initiated piece done by a child at the start of the Reception year. He had shown a real interest in how the body works, and had been looking at a lift the flap book which showed the muscles and bones beneath the skin. Clearly, this book has fascinated him, and he has replicated some of the images – you can see the bones in the hand in one of the pictures.

Graphic symbols

As well as letters and words, introduce your children to graphic symbols as part of their developing repertoire of mark making. Young children are typically very comfortable with the notion of graphic symbols – the cross on your first aid box, the green arrow pointing to the fire exit. Numbers are, of course, a very well used kind of graphic symbol that your children must learn to write. Chinese characters also offer a fantastic route into graphic symbols, as in the Practical Project below.

* * *

Practical project – Happy Chinese new year!

You will need

- Large sheets of black paper;
- Red paint;
- Easels;
- A set of the Chinese characters for 'Happy New Year' (a search on Google images brings up lots of these);
- Visit the companion website for useful internet links about the Chinese New Year.

Learning intentions

- To introduce children to a form of writing, from another culture;
- To develop understanding about other cultures and festivals;
- To help the children understand that graphic symbols can be used to communicate meaning;
- To get the children creating their own version of Chinese characters.

Instructions

Introduce the children to the idea of Chinese characters – a set of graphic symbols that 'stand for' words. Show them the characters for 'Happy New Year' and encourage them to paint their own versions of these characters. You can see an example in the photograph below. With older children you might like to talk about how the characters relate to meaning, for instance introducing them to some pictograms (i.e. the Chinese characters that are stylized drawings of what they represent).

Chinese New Year is also a great time for doing fine motor/hand to eye coordination activities, using chopsticks. Our preschool children also love to sing the Kung Hei Fat Choy song each year, and make a Chinese dragon costume in which to dance together for their parents.

In the photo, you can see how one of our 3-year-old children made a very detailed graphic representation of the Chinese characters for 'Happy New Year'. Interestingly, the boy who did this painting normally did very little mark making, preferring to focus on outdoor activities and role play. Something about the graphic nature of the symbols really struck a chord with him.

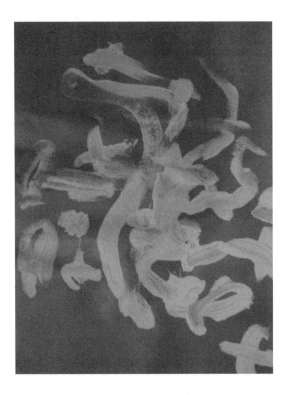

* * *

Numbers as a graphic symbol

Numbers are, of course, a special type of graphic symbol. If you look closely at modern numbers, you can see how the original graphic representations would have turned into the numbers we recognize today. Most of the time we think about writing words when we refer to children's mark making. However, it is of course also important for children to learn how to write numbers, and how to use the language of mathematics.

Boys are often particularly drawn to numbers as a starting point for their mark making. In the picture below, you can see how Álvie self-initiated a piece of writing involving numbers at the start of his time in the Reception group in a mixed age class. He has already picked up (probably from whole class sessions with the older children) that 'ten tens make one hundred'. He is using his mark making to convey the meaning that he sees within maths and numbers.

Writing and meaning at home

Those children who see their parents reading at home, and whose parents read to them, inevitably start to believe that reading is both important and pleasurable. A house that is full of books and newspapers, or at least one where parents regularly visit a library with their children, is also a key factor in early literacy. One great way we've found to encourage parents to read at home, and to support links between home and preschool, is to write a weekly blog. Our blog contains information about what the children have been doing that week. It's short and simple, but effective in communicating meaning.

Perhaps one of the very best ways in which you can help your children achieve the gift of literacy is to find strategies to encourage their parents to read to them regularly. There is a fine balance to be achieved, though, between encouraging parents and lecturing them. Tread gently when you use the following strategies:

- ✓ Ask parents to get involved, for instance in helping the children to change their book each day;
- ✓ Giving parents a reading record or reading diary within the child's folder, so that they can record what they've read together;
- ✓ Host workshops on reading stories, or more generally on how reading is taught;
- ✓ Invite parents in to your setting to share in oral presentations – poetry reading, storytelling, plays and musicals.

I Get the Link between Speaking and Writing

In this section . . .

- Find out why hearing sounds is crucial for reading and writing
- Explore ways of using stories, songs and rhymes in your setting
- Help your children understand how stories are built and written
- Get creative with your storytelling sessions

Consider this . . .

The process of learning to read and write is a bit like taking apart, and then reassembling, a piece of flat pack furniture. In order to read, the child must be able to chunk down the words into their constituent parts, that is the letter sounds, blends and syllables. This is often referred to as 'decoding' language. Then, in order to write, the child must fit those sounds back together to build the words back up again. This is often referred to as 'encoding' language. In order to pick apart and reassemble the words, a child must actually be able to hear and discriminate between the sounds *within* the words. Learning how to do this is a vital step in getting ready to read and write.

We live in an increasingly noise filled society – and many of the noises that our children hear are man-made, rather than natural, ones. A backdrop of constant radio, television, computer games or music can make it hard for children to distinguish individual sounds. Even in the outdoors, those children who live in the city will be exposed to the constant background buzz of cars, lorries and aeroplanes. It can be incredibly hard for them to focus in on talk, language and sounds. Your setting needs to offer them lots of chances to do just that. A recent report from the World Health Organization confirmed that excessive noise can impact on children's language development and cognitive functioning. See the companion website for links.

A word of warning

The current trend for teaching reading via synthetic phonics might tempt you to believe that learning to read is *only* about sound. However, it's important to understand that English is not a regular phonetic language – there are many words which break the rules, and which are impossible to spell via phonics-based methods alone. Just think for a moment of bough, cough and through. A child who relies solely on phonetic knowledge to read and write will end up misspelling many words. It's important for the teacher or practitioner to understand that words have a shape as well as being a collection of sounds, and to communicate this idea to the children. Indeed, if our plan is for our children eventually to be able to speed read, they will need to move beyond the 'sound it out' approach and learn to see words as a complete unit.

Studying sounds

Offer your children lots of opportunities to study sounds, and to learn to listen closely. This auditory discrimination is hugely important in the development of both reading and writing. Being able to pick out and identify the individual sounds within words allows children to unlock the code of written and spoken language. They also start to hear how words can have similar sounds within them, or at the end, as in rhyming words. In order to be able to distinguish letter sounds, one from another, there are three important things that the child must be able to do:

- Detection: I can hear when the sound happens;
- Discrimination: I can hear when the sound changes;
- Identification: I can hear what the sound actually is.

So long as you are sure that your children do not have physical problems with their hearing, your focus as a practitioner will be on helping the child develop the second and third aspects of auditory processing. By doing lots of activities based around hearing, studying and identifying sounds, your children will be best placed to pick out letter sounds and turn those sounds into the written word. You'll find lots of ideas below to give you inspiration.

Sound activities – instruments

- ✓ Listen to the sounds of different instruments and objects – hide the instrument or object, for instance behind a sheet, and ask the children what they can hear.
- ✓ Get the children to make shakers out of plastic bottles with different objects inside. Try: rice, beads, pasta, coins, etc. What different sounds do the different objects make?
- ✓ Ask your children to experiment with making loud sounds and quiet sounds, using different instruments. They might do this as a whole group, or individually. Which instruments are good for making really loud sounds? Which instruments tend to make sounds which are very quiet?

Sound activities – objects and resources

- ✓ Take a money box and drop coins into it, one at a time – can the children work out how many coins are in the box?
- ✓ Hide an item in a box and shake it. Ask the children to guess what the object is from the noise that it makes.
- ✓ Show the class a puppet (animals, dinosaurs) – what sound would it make? Can they create a soundtrack for the puppet?

Sound effects and sound tracking

- ✓ Talk about the sounds that animals make – identify different animals on a soundtrack CD or MP3.
- ✓ Use a listening centre with headphones to play soundtrack CDs or MP3s in your 'listening area'. Ask the children to identify the different sounds they hear on the soundtrack. Offer this as a free choice activity, as well as a whole group one.
- ✓ Visit the website www.freesound.org for some really interesting and unusual sounds. This is a creative commons site where

people share sound effects (i.e. you can use these with your children for free).

Talking and thinking about sounds

✓ Go on a listening walk and collect examples of sounds as you walk;
✓ Extend this by collecting *samples* of sounds, using a recording device. When you get back to your setting or classroom, play the sounds back and try to remember what it was that you heard;
✓ Get your children to talk about what sounds they like, and equally what sounds they don't like.

Making sounds with our bodies

✓ Stamp, splash and stomp through mud or water, echoing the sounds you make with your voices as you do it;
✓ Swish through leaves with your feet on an autumn walk;
✓ Clap, jump, wave and make accompanying sounds;
✓ Tap your hands on your knees together, on the floor, and on your tummies.

If you're in a setting where you have children with English as an additional language, invite in any parents who speak other community languages. Encourage the children to listen to the sounds in these other languages, as well as in English.

Sounds and nature

✓ Use a wide range of natural materials to create sounds – which natural materials make the best or most interesting sounds?
✓ Go for a 'sounds walk' and see how many animal sounds and sounds from nature you can hear and note down.
✓ Invite animals into your setting – this is especially easy in a rural setting like ours – we've had chicks, sheep, goats, alpacas, owls and many more to visit! In an urban area, get in touch with your local city farm if you have one close by.
✓ Encourage the children to find lots of animal sound effects for a single animal – a dog goes woof, wuff, bark, yap or yip.

Developing your listening area

Have a dedicated listening area on offer as part of your daily provision. Here are some dos and don'ts for making the most of this area:

Do

- ✓ Situate your listening area away from noisy activities;
- ✓ If possible, find some way to screen it off from distractions;
- ✓ Have a stereo with headphones, so children can listen individually;
- ✓ Have signs/symbols for 'quiet' on display – a finger to a lip, a hand to an ear.

Don't

- ✗ Have too many busy, distracting displays around your listening area;
- ✗ Let too many children use it at any one time;
- ✗ Put the instruments out for the children to use on the same day as your listening centre.

Auditory processing problems

When you're doing activities around sounds, and discriminating letter sounds within words, you may find that some of your children really seem to struggle with this. In Signpost 1 ('How talk develops'), you'll find some key symptoms to look for, which might suggest that a child has a hearing problem. However, although a difficulty in hearing sounds *might* indicate a physical problem with hearing, it may also indicate some kind of problem with the processing of auditory information. What this means is that the problem is in the *brain*, rather than in the ears.

If you notice that a child frequently displays any of the following behaviours, it may be that he has problems processing auditory information. If you are unsure, you should always refer the child for a specialist evaluation. Concerns should be raised if the child:

- ✓ Appears to have problems understanding when you give instructions;

✓ Speaks very little, or finds it hard to work out what he wants to say;
✓ Tends to lose focus, particularly when you are speaking to the group;
✓ Really struggles to hear and focus when there is lots of background noise.

 You can find a link to a helpful factsheet on Auditory Processing Disorder (APD) in the companion website.

Interestingly, children who are diagnosed as having ADHD will often display very similar symptoms to those listed above. The following strategies will support and help a child with APD, and indeed are also good practice any time you address the class:

✓ When you say something to the group, give them something to look at as well – a picture, a toy, a visual back up;
✓ Use the *sound* of your voice to give cues to the child – emphasize key words, vary the pace;
✓ When you're giving instructions, don't waffle on – keep it short and to the point;
✓ Emphasize the key words by putting stress on them;
✓ Use hand gestures to help the children understand what you're saying;
✓ Support the child as he starts the activity, to ensure that he's understood what you said;
✓ If children you teach have hearing problems, get them to sit near the front when you are addressing the whole class;
✓ When you're introducing important concepts, ideas or new skills, use lots of repetition and real life examples.

Songs, rhymes and poems

As every early years practitioner and teacher knows, songs, rhymes and poems are a wonderful way to get children tuning in to language. These forms are perfect for developing young children's language because they:

✓ Help children learn vocabulary through lots of repetition;
✓ Help children listen out for similar sounds within language – the rhymes within pat, cat, bat and mat;

✓ Have key phrases which are repeated over and over, which the child can quickly learn and repeat back;

✓ Allow the children to join in with each other, and build confidence about speaking and singing;

✓ Use simple beats and tunes, which are catchy and easy to remember;

✓ Often have matching movements or gestures, which back up the children's comprehension, make them easier to remember and encourage fine and gross motor movements;

✓ Often use alliteration, and are therefore good for picking out letter sounds ('Wee Willy Winky');

✓ Often use gradually decreasing numbers ('10 Green Bottles'), so are also great for counting activities;

✓ Have movements which improve motor skills (the 'pull, pull, clap, clap, clap' of 'Wind the Bobbin Up');

✓ Are typically known and loved by parents and practitioners, so offer a great way to link the home with the setting;

✓ Are a key part of our oral heritage, passed on from generation to generation.

There are so many great songs, rhymes and poems that you can use with your children. A quick search of the internet will bring up the words for you. Some of my favourites to use with the children are:

✓ Wind the Bobbin Up;

✓ The Wheels on the Bus;

✓ Twinkle Twinkle Little Star;

✓ Heads, Shoulders, Knees and Toes;

✓ Dingle Dangle Scarecrow;

✓ Humpty Dumpty;

✓ Incey Wincey Spider.

A quick Google search will bring up lyrics, downloadable print versions and even audio versions for you to use with your children. Visit the companion website to find links to some useful sites.

Fit in time to sing nursery rhymes throughout your sessions or your day. You could sing them at snack time, as you move around the setting, in a whole class group, in small groups, in the morning and at going home time. If it's raining, then grab your coats, wellies and umbrellas to go outside and sing 'Rain, rain, go away'! When you're using songs and rhymes with your children, encourage them to:

- ✓ Clap along with the rhythm, or tap it out on a drum;
- ✓ Join in with the words – first a single repeated phrase, gradually building up until they know the whole rhyme;
- ✓ Copy the actions as you do them, then repeat these each time you sing the song;
- ✓ Keep in time with a regular beat as you clap it or beat it out;
- ✓ Nominate their favourites, for you to sing;
- ✓ Tell you what letter sounds they can spot.

You can also play around with songs and rhymes, for instance by getting the children to:

- ✓ Sing faster, then sing slower (present this as 'singing in slow motion', then in 'super fast time');
- ✓ Sing louder, then sing quieter;
- ✓ Sing higher, then lower (accompany this by standing on tiptoes, then crouching down low).

And of course you can also use props, to spice up song time for your children. Have a box where you store your resources so that you can use them whenever you have a spare moment. In our nursery rhymes box we have the props to accompany lots of different songs, including 'Five Fat Sausages' (i.e. a saucepan and some sausages).

Rhymes

Rhymes and rhyming poems make use of phonemes, and are a great way to show children how learning one sound ('ay') can lead to learning how to write and spell many other words ('say', 'day', 'stay' and so on). When you're using poems or rhyming stories with your children:

- ✓ Encourage them to join in with the rhyming or repeated parts – 'Run, run, as fast as you can, you can't catch me I'm the ginger-bread man'.
- ✓ Do the actions together, along with the story: 'So he huffed and he puffed . . . and he huffed and he puffed'.

✓ Link rhymes to events – 'I can sing a rainbow' or 'Frosty the snowman'.
✓ Have objects that link to the rhymes to provide a visual backup for the children – for instance a toy cat, a hat, a mat, a toy rat and a bat.

Alliteration

Looking for alliteration is of course a great way to get the children hearing letter sounds within speech. After a while as an early years teacher, you will probably find yourself alliterating without even thinking about it – 'Lucy, that's a lovely little lunchbox, you lucky little thing'. Tongue twisters, such as 'She sells sea shells on the sea shore' are a great way into alliteration (and also into encouraging children to think about how they use their mouth and speech muscles to make their letter sounds).

To inspire the use of alliteration in your setting:

✓ Fill a set of boxes or bags with objects that start with the same sound, for when you are sharing letter sounds with the children. (Similar themed boxes can be used to inspire stories for older children, for instance a box full of pirate related objects and another box with toy dinosaurs, fossils and jungle plants in it.)
✓ Find opportunities to use alliterative phrases in everyday settings – simply adding an alliterative word to the children's names is a good start. So, you might have a 'Magic Mary', an 'Amazing Amy' and a 'Chipper Charlie'.
✓ Hide alliterative objects in the sand tray and ask the children what the starting letter of all the objects might be.
✓ Show the children what your mouth does when you make a 't' sound, or a 'p', and get them to make the same muscular movements.
✓ Use mirrors so that children can see what their mouth does when they make a particular sound.

The joy of stories

One of the true joys of being a teacher in the early years and primary phase (or an English teacher at secondary level), is the chance to share stories with your children. There's something very magical about a group of children mesmerized by someone reading them a story. The children feel safe, comfy and secure when they're being read a story – often little children will lie down, flop backwards, or even doze off.

If our hope is that one day our little children will progress to writing stories of their own, we need to show them how magical the story world can be. One of the key skills of the early years practitioner or teacher is to be able to tell a story in a way that engrosses and captivates the children. The best storytellers bring the story to life, by using every skill at their disposal. At first, it can feel a bit silly going over the top with the kind of voice that you use, or making the faces of the different characters. But the more lively and multisensory your telling of the story is, the more entranced your children will be by the story worlds you create. To get the very best out of stories in your setting:

- ✓ Give the children time to fall *completely silent* before you tell a story – use a pause and some non-verbal interventions to encourage them to give you their attention.
- ✓ Use big books whenever you can, so that all the children can see the words and pictures.
- ✓ Hold the book facing the group, and to one side of you, so that you can read it easily and the children can see it the right way up.
- ✓ Alternatively, hold the book in front of you, and learn the skill of reading upside down.
- ✓ Make the most of tone – it really is impossible to overdo the use of tone with this age group. Sound *really* excited, *really* scared, *really* angry.
- ✓ Modulate the speed of your voice, to show where excitement is building up, and when there is a calmer section. Use a fast, breathless pace to show urgency or fear, and a slow, soft pace for quieter, calmer bits of the story.
- ✓ Play around with your volume levels as well – if you spot that the children are losing focus, try leaning forwards slightly and speaking really quietly, to encourage them to listen closely.

✓ Use facial expressions, both to help you communicate meaning and emotion to the children, but also to encourage you to add tone into your voice. If you make a surprised face, you will find that this really helps you to achieve a surprised tone of voice.

Consider using a large-scale puppet to help you tell the story, or perhaps even play one of the characters in the story. This can help you feel a bit less silly about doing funny voices and using plenty of tone. It's also very captivating for the children, who are quite happy to go along with the 'fiction' of a puppet helping you tell a story.

Interactive stories

Modern day children are being brought up in a highly interactive world, one that is fundamentally different to that of only 20 or 30 years ago. Digital television, the internet, electronics, computer games and computer based toys – all now offer a two way flow of information and ideas to our children. For instance the story book that 'reads' to you when you press a button, or the toy that asks you to respond to an instruction ('bop it!'); similarly, the red dot that pops up on the TV screen, or the touch screen technology of a handheld console or a mobile phone. Modern children are used to interactivity, and there is very little point in us complaining how children 'used to' concentrate better or manage on a single hour of children's TV a day.

Take on board the interactive nature of the modern world by finding ways to make your storytelling sessions an interactive, multisensory experience. You'll find that this is particularly important if you work with very young children, or have some children who struggle with their concentration levels. Develop the ability to 'read' your group so that you quickly realize when they are beginning to lose their focus and you need to make the story more engaging. Look out for signs such as fidgeting, looking away and starting to bother each other. Learn to read the story with one eye, while simultaneously reading the group's levels of focus with the other. It sounds hard to do, but with practice and experience you get the hang of it.

There are many ways to make a story interactive as you tell it. You might:

- ✓ Get all the children to become characters in the story, for instance standing up to 'climb' the trees and 'swinging' through the vines in a story about the jungle.
- ✓ Add props to engage their interest, for instance some straw, twigs and bricks for the children to see or handle or even blow over while you are telling the story of the Three Little Pigs.
- ✓ Add 'invisible' props to encourage an imaginative response, for instance you could ask the children to hold and stroke a frightened cat, while telling them the story of *The Lighthouse Keeper's Lunch* (Ronda and David Armitage, Scholastic, 2007).
- ✓ Add costumes, such as hats and gloves, either for the children, or for yourself. For instance asking for volunteers to wear the clothes while telling the story of '*The Smartest Giant in Town*' (Julia Donald and Axel Scheffler, Macmillan, 2003).
- ✓ Encourage the children to add 'sound effects' – for instance all joining in as the Giant says '*Fee Fi Fo Fum*', or making the sound of the Billy Goats Gruff trip trapping across the bridge.
- ✓ Do some team storytelling – where one person tells the story, while the second person makes the voices, points at the pictures or does the actions.

Of course, you can also bring stories to life after the event. For example, taking the story of *The Lighthouse Keeper's Lunch*, you might make the lunch and create a basket and pulley system to get the lunch across to the lighthouse. You might also challenge the children to think of ways to keep those pesky seagulls at bay.

With older children who are starting to write, encourage them to respond to stories through different written forms, and to interact with the characters within them. In the sample shown in the image below, you can see how the teacher has got the child to write to the mouse to ask for help in pulling up the enormous turnip. The child was aged 5-years-old and was in the Reception group within a mixed year group class.

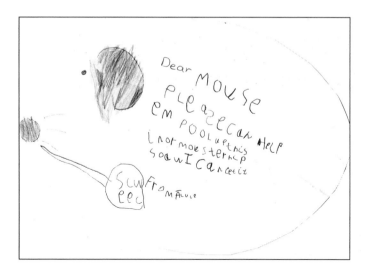

Interestingly, you can see here how the child is using the *sound* of language to help him know how to write the words. His writing says:

> 'Dear mouse, please can you help me pull up this enor-mous turnip so I can eat it. From Álvie'. The mouse is going 'scweec' ('squeak'). At first, particularly in their free writing, the children rely on the *sound* of words to try and work out how they are spelt.

I Feel Confident about Communicating 6

In this section . . .

- Help your children build their confidence in communicating
- Encourage your children to express their opinions
- Use drama activities to boost self esteem
- Learn how to use the 'Role of the Expert' to improve confidence
- Consider how to use marking in a constructive way

Consider this . . .

Communication, by its very nature, involves more than one person. This book can only communicate ideas and information because of its relationship to you, the person reading it. You act as an audience for what I'm saying – you bring it to life and give it meaning. If this text sat on a shelf, gathering dust, it would communicate nothing to anybody, even though the words were there inside its pages. When we communicate, whether through speech or through writing, the way that our audience responds and reacts is absolutely vital to the experience.

In many ways, writing is a risky business, requiring a great deal of confidence from the person doing the writing. When you create a piece of writing, you put your own thoughts, ideas and opinions down on paper, for some kind of audience to read. But what if the audience doesn't like what you've written, or how you've written it? As educators, we are often required to sit in judgement on our children's writing, to see whether it matches up to 'expected levels'. The way that we respond and react to their efforts can either boost or damage their self-confidence and their motivation to communicate through writing in the future.

When we're writing, most of us have a kind of 'internal editor' sitting on our shoulder. This is that nagging inner voice which tells us 'you can't say that' or 'that sounds really silly'. But listening to this voice stifles a writer's confidence, so take care that you don't become a kind of internal editor for the children you teach. Our ultimate aim must be for our children to become confident communicators, who feel inspired to write in order to express themselves, and to share their ideas. This takes their writing one step beyond simply meeting targets, and turns it into a valid act of communication.

Building confident communicators

Each child you work with is a unique individual, with a personality all of his or her own. Some children will be confident and outgoing, others will be cripplingly shy; some will prefer to sit back and let others take the lead, still others will be the leader in every peer group situation. A confident attitude can be influenced by many factors. Certainly, where children have secure early attachments – caring parents, a strong family network – this helps boost their brain development and makes them feel more confident. But other factors play a part – birth order is often key, with the oldest sibling being more confident and outgoing.

The notion that it's important for children to develop 'emotional intelligence' has come to the fore a great deal in recent years. The idea that learning is affected by the child's social and emotional state has also been recognized in the Social and Emotional Aspects of Learning (SEAL) materials. Ours is a busy, stressful society, and children's mental health is often a fragile thing. Well-known educators such as Anthony Seldon question how we can ensure a happy society, and put 'happiness lessons' on the curriculum at their schools.

It's worth thinking about what we mean by confidence. A self-confident child (or indeed adult):

- ✓ Is self-assertive;
- ✓ Has high self-esteem;
- ✓ Feels that their ideas matter;
- ✓ Is happy to express their opinions and speak out;
- ✓ Is resilient when things go wrong and can 'bounce back' quickly from set backs;
- ✓ Knows how to handle criticism, and how to put it to good use.

You can support your children and build their confidence in lots of different ways. However, practitioners and teachers can also *damage* young children's confidence and self-esteem very easily indeed (often unintentionally). If you think back to when you were at school you may well have had teachers who damaged your self-confidence, perhaps without even realizing they were doing it. The list of dos and don'ts below should help you think about how you can support your children in building their self-confidence:

Do

✓ Listen with interest to what they have to say (and even if you're *not* particularly interested at that precise moment, at least *look* like you are);

✓ Encourage them to develop what they say through subtle and open-ended questioning techniques;

✓ Join in with their play and enjoy the time you spend with them;

✓ Take their emotions seriously, rather than brushing them aside;

✓ Set targets or activities that stretch them, but which they can access and at which they can succeed;

✓ Respect their interests, and find activities that fit well with these;

✓ Acknowledge that sometimes you find things difficult, for instance talking about how it can be tricky to find the right words when you're writing on the board;

✓ Let your children know that it is okay to take risks, to make mistakes and to get things wrong;

✓ Let them try new things, even if they are not yet 'good' at them;

✓ Encourage them to be independent learners, and also to be independent in self-care;

✓ Remember that dismissive comments and difficult situations affect us much more deeply when we are young.

Don't

✗ Laugh *at* them if they do something wrong;

✗ Use dismissive language – words such as 'silly', 'rubbish';

✗ Tell them what to do all the time, using lists of instructions and demands;

  × Even if they are being particularly difficult, or you're having a bad day, don't let your emotions come through in your tone of voice or facial expressions;
  × Use lots of closed questions, which don't allow them to express their ideas;
  × Set targets that they simply cannot reach;
  × Nit pick or nag, even when you're feeling stressed by your class;
  × Complain when they make a mess, if it is a valid part of their learning;
  × Brush off their concerns – make sure you take them seriously, and acknowledge when they are worried or nervous about something (even if you feel they are being 'silly').

Above all else, when you work with children you need to be very conscious indeed not to have 'favourites'. Although you might recoil at the idea that this could apply to you, it is important to admit that you probably like some children more than you like others. Because if you don't admit this it can subconsciously affect the way you behave with different children. Ask yourself (and be honest):

  • Do I pick some children more often than others to answer questions during whole class/group time?
  • If I'm honest, are there some children I prefer, and does this perhaps come out in the way that I treat them?
  • Similarly, do I allow any negative feelings about the children to come out in the way that I talk to them and interact with them?
  • Am I ever dismissive of some children's ideas, or do I see less value in what some children say than in others?

The secret when working with children is to acknowledge your personal feelings, but to take a professional approach. In other words, you must try your hardest not to let your feelings affect your behaviour towards them.

Using praise and target setting

We all like to be told that we've done something well, but to be valuable, praise needs to be genuine and really well focused. Similarly, we all benefit from having targets towards which we can work, but again these need to be clear and realistic for us to achieve. It's important to realize that you won't create a self-confident child by simply telling her that everything she does is great (no matter whether it is or not). Because when she comes up against challenges and critiques in later life, as she inevitably will, she won't know how to cope with them. In addition, research has shown that it is far more effective in terms of motivation to praise a child for the *effort* that he puts into things, than for the level of *achievement* he manages to attain.

Being able to praise a child for his effort relies on your knowledge of your individual children. Some of your children may be able to achieve a great piece of writing, without much effort at all. For other children, a single sentence could represent a huge milestone. Similarly, your use of targets will depend a great deal on the kind of child with whom you're working. Some children benefit from quite a hefty push, enjoying the challenge of the teacher saying 'you could do this better'. Other children, particularly those with some kind of special educational needs, will crumble unless you are very careful in how you phrase any constructive criticism.

Making the most of praise

When you're praising a piece of work that a child has done, try to avoid vague generalizations about how 'good' or not it might be. Try not to comment on the child's individual aptitude (words like 'clever' and 'intelligent'). These kind of comments don't help the child reflect on his work, nor improve it next time round. For instance:

> *'Wow, what a great picture, aren't you clever!'*

Instead, the best praise gives specific, detailed comments which highlight exactly what it is about the child's work that is so good:

> *'I really like the way that you've used the red paint to show how the volcano is overflowing.'*

Similarly, when you're praising a child's mark making or writing, avoid generalized comments such as:

> *'That's such a great poem, aren't you a clever girl.'*

Instead, talk specifically about what the child has done that works well:

> *'I love the way you've used alliteration in your poem to echo the sounds of the fireworks.'*

Setting targets

Alongside the use of praise to boost your children's confidence, you can also give targets for future improvement. A useful ratio is to give one target for improvement, for every three positive comments you make about what the child has done. (The 'Three Stars and a Wish' approach as explained below.) Make sure that the targets you set:

- ✓ Are clear and specific;
- ✓ Involve improving one aspect, rather than lots;
- ✓ Are realistic and achievable;
- ✓ Are supportive and kindly phrased;
- ✓ Encourage the child to push herself that bit further.

Practising using praise and targets

Perhaps the best way to improve your use of praise and targets is to practise using them. Below you will see a piece of child-initiated writing, done by a 5-year-old who is already a fluent reader. Consider how you might respond to this piece of writing:

- ✓ What would you say to the child about the positive aspects of what she has written?
- ✓ What could she do next time round to improve her writing even further?
- ✓ Clearly, there are a number of technical issues with this piece of writing – which one would you pick out for the child to work on and improve?
- ✓ What are the 'next steps' for this child to move her on in terms of her writing?
- ✓ Would you write your comments on the piece itself, or do you think it would work better to chat to her about what she's done?

Marking writing

As children learn to write more fluently, you will begin to give evaluative comments on their writing to help them improve. The key to ensuring that this process is confidence building, rather than soul destroying, is to strike a balance between targeted praise and constructive criticism. Clearly, this will vary according to the needs of the child.

Most teachers will have worked with children whose writing is incredibly weak, and strewn with errors. Intuitively, we realize that to highlight every error within a hard-won piece of writing could devastate the child. Marking needs to be a constructive dialogue between teacher and child, that is supportive but which still pushes the child to do that little bit better next time around.

In the 'old days', marking involved putting a big red tick or cross at the end of a child's work and perhaps a brief comment. However, it is now understood that this kind of marking is pretty much pointless. Instead, we try to ensure that our assessment is *for learning,* that it informs and supports the learning as well as simply assessing it. For marking to be effective in helping a child improve her writing, it needs to:

✓ Give specific details about what works well within the piece;
✓ Set a clear target for future improvement, which is understood by the child;

✓ Explain to the child how she can improve on this aspect (for instance asking her to practise spelling a misspelt word in the back of her book);
✓ Actually be read by the child – set aside time for this when handing back writing that you have marked.

Visual marking

A useful technique for older children is to use a highlighter pen to identify both the aspects of the writing that work well, and also the areas which you want the child to target next. Use the same colours every time you mark – for instance pink for the good bits, and green for the bits the child could improve. Make sure that your children (and their parents) understand why you are using these different colours, and what they actually mean.

Three stars and a wish

This is a lovely technique for marking writing which allows you to identify what has worked well in a piece, as well as giving a target for future improvement. The 'three stars' are three aspects of the writing that work well; the 'wish' is the area that you'd like the student to work on further. Your children can also use this approach when doing peer assessment.

My opinion matters

Part of being self-confident is feeling as though your ideas and opinions matter, and that you're going to be taken seriously. Find ways to let your children express their opinions, and influence the choices that are made within your setting or school. For instance they could:

✓ Choose what they want to play with, for instance through a 'choices board';
✓ Tell you about their favourite resources, and about any new ones that they would like to see;
✓ Put forward their ideas at circle time, or as part of a school council;

✓ Have an influence on the way that you structure your day, for instance deciding when you tell a whole class story;
✓ Share their thoughts about what matters to them, for instance through showing a favourite toy at Show and Tell;
✓ Share their news with you every Monday morning;
✓ Choose a topic for their writing, or select some questions that they want answered in class.

Open-ended discussions

One of the key ways in which you can support your children in feeling that they are important, and that their ideas have value, is through the use of open-ended discussion techniques. This is a key skill for early years practitioners and teachers to learn, but it is surprisingly difficult to do. Often, teachers and practitioners use a verbal style involving lots of instructions and directions ('*tidy up*', '*put on your coats*'). They also tend to use plenty of closed questions ('*who has finished their work?*') and indeed rhetorical questions as well ('*why are you being so noisy?*'). This may be because of an urge to 'get through' the learning, to keep the children 'under control' or simply because it's become a matter of habit over time.

In the early years, open-ended discussions are often referred to as 'sustained shared thinking', that is a conversation between the adult and child in which you work together to support and extend the child's thinking skills. In order to understand more about this approach, it's useful to think about the different kinds of verbal styles we might use in the early years setting.

Instructions/Directions: The teacher or practitioner makes statements to the child about what he should do. The child is expected to comply with what he's being asked to do, rather than questioning what the teacher has said. Sometimes the practitioner will *phrase* these instructions as a rhetorical question ('*can you build me a tower?*') but he is, in reality, actually giving an instruction or direction.

For example:

> '*Tommy, I want you to build me a tower with ten blocks.*'
> '*Find the circle in this picture.*'

'We've finished building our Little Pigs' house, now we're all going to tidy up the straw.'

Closed questions: The teacher or practitioner asks questions that only have one 'correct' answer, usually requiring a short one or two word response. The child is 'right' if they answer correctly, and 'wrong' if their answer is incorrect. Closed questions have their place – as a test of the knowledge or skills that a child already has. However, they tend to shut down any chance of a conversation, or of higher order thinking.

For example:

'How many blocks are in your tower, Tommy?'
'Can you find three different shapes in this picture?'
'What is the first house in The Three Little Pigs made of?'

Open questions: These are questions that open up a discussion, and which do not have a single 'correct' answer. They are often to do with feelings, opinions or ideas. There is no right or wrong answer: whatever the child says can be valid and valued.

For example:

'What's that you're making, Tommy? It looks very interesting, could you tell me about it?'
'Who can tell me what their favourite thing is about this picture?'
'I was thinking we could make some houses, like in the Three Little Pigs story that we read earlier. Has anyone got any ideas about what they would like to make their house from?'

Open-ended questioning is valuable because:

✓ It encourages a greater use of lateral thinking, and of higher order thinking skills such as theorizing and deduction;
✓ It can help you find ways to solve a problem, together with the children;
✓ It allows you to help the children understand a concept more clearly;

✓ It builds the children's confidence in feeling that their ideas and opinions matter;

✓ It helps us consider the 'big questions' of life – it is a philosophical technique;

✓ It allows the adult to build on what the children already know, moving the discussion in the most appropriate direction.

Sustained shared thinking

When you observe children's play, and judge that it would be useful for you to become involved, you can use open-ended questioning and discussion techniques to move the thinking and ideas forwards. This is a process, which will be different each time, in which you might use some or all of the following techniques:

Tune in
Listen carefully to what the child is saying
'Read' his body language
Watch his play before you intervene

Take an interest
Give the child your full attention
Make eye contact and smile
Ask open questions about their play

Encourage them to elaborate or summarize
Say:
'I'd really love to hear more about that'
'That's very interesting, could you show me again?'
'So you made that bit first did you?'

Share your experiences and ideas
Tell a story about when you did something similar
Offer a suggestion as to how the child might do something

Use focused praise and targets
Highlight what the child has done well
Suggest something she might try next

Offer fresh perspectives
Identify an alternative viewpoint on the issue
Encourage the child to think about what others might do/feel/say/think

Model your thought processes
Use vocabulary around thinking when you talk with the child
Explain your own processes when you're thinking

This last step is known as 'metacognition' – the process of think-ing about what we're thinking, of being aware of our own thought processes.

Group activities and circle time

One of the very best formats for boosting confidence and self-esteem is working in a group. Within a group, we can share and develop our ideas, work together to achieve things, solve problems, boost relation-ships and so on. Circle time offers a great chance for your children to share their ideas with the group as a whole. It can also help you boost the confidence of your quieter children. The format of a circle is a very inclusive one – everyone can see each other, and we can easily share our thoughts and ideas.

When using a circle to share ideas:

✓ Make the children stand in a proper circular shaped circle – encourage them to think about the structure of a circle and what it means to them;
✓ Allow children to 'pass' if they don't want to contribute – never put them on the spot or force a quiet child to take part;
✓ Use circles of different sizes – sometimes your whole class or group, but sometimes a smaller circle so that any shy children are more likely to contribute;
✓ Praise the children for good 'circle time behaviours' such as lis-tening carefully, taking turns and so on.

Here are some suggestions for simple circle time activities:

✓ Talking Ted – each child holds the teddy and tells the group one thing.
✓ Show the group an animal – as they pass it around, they should say one thing about the animal, for instance when passing

round a toy cow, they could say *'a cow is black and white'*, *'a cow gives us milk'*.

✓ My news – one thing they did over the weekend.

✓ Free association – give the children a theme, for instance *'water'* and ask them to say a word that links to the theme – cold, hot, pool, tap, hose, etc.

✓ Pass a tambourine around, as each child gets it, they tap out their name.

✓ Ask the children to each tell you their favourite thing, based on a theme that you or the children choose. For instance my favourite TV programme, my favourite food, my favourite toy.

✓ Sing a song together, and all do the actions.

✓ Play 'leader of the band': one volunteer shuts his eyes, while you choose a 'leader'. That child leads the band in a series of movements – tapping their hands on their knees, clapping their hands, tapping their shoulders, etc. The volunteer must try to guess who the 'leader of the band' is; the rest of the children must try to change at the same moment as the leader, to stop their identity from being revealed.

✓ Pass a toy animal around the circle, for instance a toy guinea pig, but ask the children to act as though it is real. Encourage the children to handle it gently, comfort it and so on. You can also do this with an invisible pet.

✓ And of course, all the old favourites, such as Chinese Whispers, Wink Murder, Fruit Salad, Simon Says and so on.

The 'role of the expert'

The 'role of the expert' is a fantastic drama technique which is great for boosting children's confidence, and encouraging them to take an independent and mature approach to their learning. It is also sometimes referred to as the 'mantle of the expert'. This technique is most useful within role play and drama activities. With older children you can use it as a way into other subjects as well, for instance science ('forensic experts', 'scientists at a government laboratory'). The idea of the technique is that:

✓ The children assume the role of an expert of some kind – a doctor, a vet, a police officer, a superhero;

✓ They play this role within the drama, for instance playing in role as a doctor in a hospital-based role play scenario;

✓ They take on the attributes and attitudes of the character they are playing;

✓ They also use the kind of language and vocabulary that this expert would use in real life.

The benefits of the 'role of the expert' include:

✓ The children tend to take on more mature attitudes and responses while playing within the role;

✓ You can ask them to do mark making or writing activities that this 'expert' would do (for instance making notes about a patient);

✓ The role they have taken on can boost their confidence through the idea of becoming someone else, who is an 'expert' on a subject or area;

✓ The teacher can help control the role play from inside the drama by taking on a role within the scenario.

I Feel Inspired to Make Marks

In this section . . .

- Give your children a real reason for their writing
- Inspire your children through imaginative approaches
- Boost motivation to write for all children, including the boys
- Use provocations and challenges to make writing exciting
- Find ideas for themes that inspire mark making

Consider this . . .

As we move ever further into the digital age, writing with a pencil and paper as opposed to writing via typing on a keyboard becomes an ever less common event in our daily lives. Even though I'm a professional writer, it's fairly rare for me to actually put pen to paper as opposed to putting fingers to keyboard. Similarly, the 'snail mail' communication done via letters and postcards seems rather slow and old fashioned now that we have email and text messaging. What all this means is that your children are less and less likely to see their parents or carers putting pen to paper at home. In turn, it becomes ever more important for them to see practitioners and teachers doing this in the early years setting.

Throughout their years of education, it's absolutely crucial for children to have a good reason for writing. We simply *must* encourage them to feel an urge to write, rather than seeing it as a chore, if our hope is for them to become skilled and avid writers. Because writing is hard work, especially for those children who have any kind of literacy related special needs. So often in schools, we tell our students that they have to write to meet targets, or because we, the teachers, insist that they must. But this is not a genuine reason to write. A piece of writing only comes to life when it has a real audience – an interested reader – to interact with it. If we want our children to achieve their best, they really must feel motivated to communicate with others, through making marks and using words.

Inspirational mark making

There are certain key features that tend to inspire children (and indeed people of any age) to get engaged with an educational activity. When you're looking to create truly inspirational mark making activities, make sure that the activity, or the resources that accompany it, fulfil some or all of the following criteria:

Big or long	Colourful	Multisensory
Unusual/unexpected	Contrasting	Real, relevant
Open ended	True to life	Arising from interests
Based on experiences	Secretive	All about me!

Here are some ideas about how you can utilize these techniques with your children:

- ✓ **Big/Long:** Make the writing area unusually big or long – so that it offers the children a giant, super sized canvas. For instance you could wrap a climbing frame completely in lining paper, so that the children can create the outline of a 'castle' on it.
- ✓ **Unusual:** Get the children writing on an unusual backdrop – a wall, a large sheet of cardboard, a bed sheet, the ground. Set up the activity in an unusual place – under a desk, on the ceiling, as a treasure hunt around the school grounds.
- ✓ **Colourful/contrasting:** Black and white, or black and silver, both work well for writing about space. Red and black make a great graphic contrast symbolizing fire or danger.
- ✓ **Multisensory:** Feel sandpaper letter shapes, in a feely bag, to see if the children can identify them by touch alone. Get your children splashing in the water or playing in the snow, and then writing about what they felt.
- ✓ **Arising from interests:** A focus on 'superheroes', with a 'superhero den' on offer, for children who show a fascination

with these characters, or a focus on writing cartoons for children who love comics.

- ✓ **Based on experiences:** A trip to a museum, a movie that they've seen recently, a diary kept while on holiday – the immediacy and vibrancy of the experience makes the writing feel real and purposeful.
- ✓ **Secretive:** Children love the idea of things being hidden, and having to be kept secret. An envelope on the desks, saying 'Do not Open' will inspire all sorts of interest and engagement.
- ✓ **All about me!:** We all love to talk about ourselves, and writing is the epitome of something that is all about me. Even if we are not writing about ourselves, as in an autobiographical piece, our writing is still an expression of who we are and what we think and feel.

Below are some examples of writing inspired by some of the above features.

Arising from interests/Based on experiences

In this piece of self-initiated writing, the Reception aged child had been to see the Disney Pixar film WALL-E. He has been inspired to draw the characters from the film, and write about how WALL-E 'saff his pinit' ('saves his planet'). He has also labelled the different parts of the characters, including 'arms' and 'bonit' ('bonnet').

Multisensory/Based on experiences/All about me!

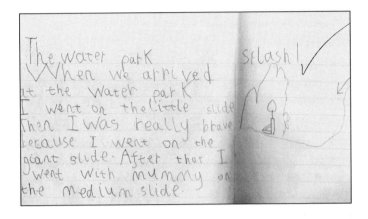

This piece of writing was done in a 'holiday diary', at the end of Year 1, where the teacher had asked the children to keep a diary of what they did during their holiday. You can sense the thrill the child felt, and the sense of urgency in trying to get across how it felt to go to the water park.

Creating a writing area

Show that writing really matters within your setting or classroom by having an area dedicated solely to writing. Think carefully about how you will set this out, and the kind of resources you might have on offer. It's a good idea to have a unit in which to store all the various resources. Make your area look quite 'grown up' and a bit like an office if you can. You'll probably find that you have to tidy this area up after each session, particularly at preschool age, and preferably with the children helping you. By keeping the area tidy, and the resources in tip-top condition, you show that you view writing as important and worthwhile.

Writing area checklist

 You can find a downloadable copy of this checklist in the companion website.

Resource	Tick
Postcards	☐
Pencils, pens, felt tips, biros, markers	☐
Letter writing paper	☐
Envelopes in all different sizes	☐
Pads and notebooks	☐
Paper in a variety of types, sizes, colours and textures	☐
Clipboards – A4 and also small size	☐
Scissors	☐
Post it notes	☐
Sticky labels	☐
Comics and magazines	☐
A postbox	☐
A word bank	☐
A set of magnetic letters/words	☐
Alphabet stencils	☐
Bulldog clips, paper clips	☐
Stapler	☐
Hole punch	☐
Treasury tags	☐
Rulers	☐
Glue sticks	☐
Sellotape in a dispenser	☐
Masking tape	☐
Pre-printed forms	☐
Child's dictionary	☐
Folders	☐
Telephone	☐
Mini whiteboards	☐

Make sure that you model the use of your writing area for your children. This might be as simple as sitting down at the desk and doing some writing of your own (perhaps making notes to go in a child's learning journey or profile). By seeing you writing, and using writing to communicate meaning, your children learn that writing is of value and has a valid purpose.

Change the focus of your writing area regularly, to keep it fresh and exciting for the children. Use the children's interests to help you decide what focus to take. You could try:

- ✓ **An 'Author's Table':** This works well for a focus on writing fiction, or on a particular author. Take photos of the children in your class and laminate them, then offer these as 'character cards' for your children to use in their stories.
- ✓ **An 'Historical Table':** Use tea bags to stain paper for an aged feel. Offer the children scrolls of paper to write on, and feather quills and ink to write with.
- ✓ **A 'Superhero Table':** Have a selection of superhero magazines and comics on offer. Laminate superhero cards, to give the children inspiration for characters to go into their writing. Make a 'superhero passport' with details of the hero.
- ✓ **A 'Disney Table':** Have a selection of books with fairy tales and other Disney stories available. Laminate a set of Disney character pictures for the children to use in their story writing. A mirror works well for encouraging the children to put themselves into the story. Write on the mirror in dry wipe pen: *'Mirror, mirror, on the wall, who is the fairest of them all?'*

You can use your writing area both for free writing, and also for more focused or adult-directed activities.

Making writing real

Think about times during your sessions or lessons when you genuinely need to use writing or make marks for a *real* purpose. A routine for registration is a very good example of this – you genuinely need to know who is in the session. Depending on their age and level of skill at writing, your children might:

- ✓ Make marks to self-register, for instance on a wipe-clean board;
- ✓ Write up their names on an interactive whiteboard;
- ✓ Slide their names onto the 'sad' or 'happy' columns on your interactive whiteboard;
- ✓ Velcro laminated name strips to a felt board;

✓ Help you call out the names on the register, while you mark who is present and absent.

Modelling writing

Find lots of ways to let your children see you using writing in real life situations. By modelling writing for the children you show that it is a valuable skill, and that we use it all the time in our day-to-day lives. You might:

✓ Get the children to sit with you and comment/join in while you update their learning journeys or foundation stage profiles;
✓ Jot down observations about the children's play on post it notes and ask the children to help you add these into their profiles;
✓ Sit with children to mark their writing, and to write positive comments and targets for improvement;
✓ Take 'orders' at snack time on an order pad;
✓ Model the use of writing frames on your interactive white-board to show the children how a particular form of writing works;
✓ Have a postbox in which you post messages to your children, and they can post messages to you.

As you write, talk about the intellectual processes that are going on in your head. This use of metacognition – talking about our thinking – is very important in the development of higher order thinking skills.

Using ICT

The modern day world revolves around technologies such as the internet, email and smart phones. Just a couple of decades ago we had to communicate via letters, and look up information in an encyclopaedia. Now it's a quick email dashed off and sent, or a quick Google search to find out the facts. The young children we teach have been brought up with these new technologies – they are an integral part of their world, and something that has always been there for them. This means that Information and Communications Technology (ICT) plays a key part in showing your children that writing has a real purpose and value in the world.

You might use ICT to:

- ✓ Write a regular Blog entry, with your children contributing their ideas while you type them up;
- ✓ Create a website on which you feature samples of the children's writing;
- ✓ Make PowerPoints together with the children, to show their knowledge on a subject;
- ✓ Draw tracks or mazes for your Bee-Bots or other remote control toys;
- ✓ Use online games to improve literacy – the BBC website is a great place for these;
- ✓ Watch an online animation of correct letter formation, or of how to form cursive joins;
- ✓ Model writing for and with your class, on your interactive whiteboard.

Once children are writing, ICT can offer a real lifeline to those who struggle, particularly those children who have issues with handwriting, who struggle with spelling or who have Dyslexia.

*   *   *

Practical project – A trip to the shops

You will need

- ✓ A large sheet of paper;
- ✓ Marker pens;
- ✓ A good reason to visit the shops (see below).

Learning intentions

- ✓ Helping the children understand that writing has a purpose;
- ✓ Linking learning to a writing structure that the children may have seen at home – although many parents probably don't hand write much at home, most of them will at some point have written a shopping list.

Instructions

At preschool, our most recent trip was to a local garden centre. We won the Alan Titchmarsh award from the Royal Horticultural Society (RHS) for our preschool garden and allotment. This meant we had an envelope full of vouchers to spend, and a good reason to spend them. Before our trip, we wrote a shopping list with the children, with the adults modelling the writing process. We thought about what we might need or want to buy. We definitely wanted some high quality spades to use on our allotment.

Your trip to the shops might be for something simple, such as fruit and vegetables for snack times, or something unusual, such as a new animal for your school farm. You could look up information with the children about prices and shop opening times on the internet or in a local directory, before your trip.

You can expand and extend this activity by writing shopping and other lists at different times of the year: a shopping list for Santa Claus, a packing list for going away on holiday in the summer, a list of questions for the children to ask the teacher they will have next year and so on.

* * *

Using provocations

A 'provocation' sounds like something really complicated, but all it really means is a challenge or a puzzle. The question – *how can we solve this?* – is used to inspire the children's learning. As they work together to answer the question, they talk, they extend their thinking, and they have a real and valid reason to make marks. Your provocation could be:

- ✓ A letter which the class receives from a storybook character who has a problem. For instance the Prince in Cinderella saying he cannot find the princess who left her shoe behind.
- ✓ A situation that needs resolving, for instance someone has been overfeeding the class pet, with the children having to think up ways to stop this happening in future.
- ✓ An object or prop that has been left behind in the classroom – for instance a handbag. How can we work out whose bag it is?
- ✓ A 'scene of the crime' type activity, for example the class toy has been stolen and some evidence has been left behind. How can we figure out 'whodunnit'?

* * *

 ## Practical project – Animal rescue

You will need

- ✓ Toy animals;
- ✓ Bandages and sellotape/masking tape;

✓ Plasters;

✓ Boxes of 'medication';

✓ A first aid kit;

✓ Clipboards and pencils for the vets to take notes;

✓ An old changing mat;

✓ A baby bath or bowl with water in;

✓ Cloths and sponges for wiping;

✓ Some white 'vet' coats if available;

✓ A diary and pencils/pens;

✓ A telephone;

✓ Boxes or animal containers/carriers;

✓ Resources for the rescue – a rope, a stepladder, a net, etc.

Learning intentions

✓ To develop the children's fine motor skills;

✓ To challenge the children to think 'outside the box';

✓ To use a dramatic context as a basis for developing writing and thinking skills.

Instructions

Set up an 'Animal Rescue Centre' in your role play area – a place where injured animals can be brought to be treated. (The children may be familiar with the concept of 'animal rescue' from watching television programmes such as *Dora the Explorer* and those featuring her cousin *Diego*, or from real life animal rescue documentaries on television.)

Have a variety of areas on offer within your Animal Rescue Centre: an area to clean and wash any injured animals; an area for treating them and bandaging their injured limbs (great for fine motor skills); a Reception area with a telephone and diary where you can take calls about injured animals, and note down the details when they are brought in; a surgery area, with clipboards for the vets to write on their notes. You might also have a quiet area for the animals to rest in boxes, once they have been treated. The children can of course free play within their animal rescue centre as well as trying to solve the provocation below.

The provocation

Set up a situation for the provocation ahead of time, by placing one of your toy animals in a tree or in a similar high up position. Have a variety of resources on hand for your 'animal rescuers' to request – a rope, a step ladder. Make a phone call to your animal rescue team, from a passer-by who has seen the animal in trouble – can they come and help you with the rescue?

An extension

We tied our 'animal rescue' theme in to a visit from a 'Rainforest Adventure' group who showed the children a variety of exotic creatures such as a snake, a spider and a giant snail. We also had a visit from a group who brought in owls and other birds of prey to show the children, and for them to handle.

∗   ∗   ∗

Writing in creative contexts

As well as 'real' writing for a real purpose (e.g. making a shopping list), writing can also take place in a real way but within a creative context. The ability of young children to enter the fictional world means you can offer them experiences, places and opportunities that they treat as real. These may be places and experiences that they would never have access to outside of the nursery or school environment. The creative art forms of dance, drama, music and art all tend to be hugely inspirational for children. These creative forms are great for boosting their self-confidence, for instance through performing to a small audience. They are also ideal for self-expression. You might be:

- ✓ Making marks to music, or to the sound of percussion instruments – how can we represent these sounds or beats using a pen or a paint brush? How can we show the lengths of the different sounds?
- ✓ Using dance to inspire mark making, for instance dancing on a large sheet of paper with paint on your feet.
- ✓ Acting out scenarios that involve writing, for instance a parking attendant puts a parking ticket on the role play car, or the prince writes some invitations to the Ball.
- ✓ Working together on an art project designed to communicate a message – for instance a mosaic of your school motto, or a new design or logo for your school or preschool uniform.

At preschool, our children particularly love our weekly Yoga session. This is taught by a Yoga teacher, who uses stories and dramatized scenarios to encourage the children to try out the different Yoga moves. For instance the story of The Very Hungry Caterpillar with the caterpillar coming out of the egg and eating the various foods.

'Real' role-play environments

Your role play area offers a fantastic environment for purposeful mark making. You can relate the way you set up the area to a theme you're using in class, to the children's interests or to a particular skill or idea you want to introduce. It can be a good idea to talk with your children first about a new role play area. Your discussion might include talking about:

- ✓ What kind of things people might do in this setting;
- ✓ The kind of vocabulary that they might use;
- ✓ The kind of characters we might meet here and what jobs or roles they would have;
- ✓ What sort of writing might happen within this area;
- ✓ Whether the children have been to this type of setting in real life, and what their experiences of it were.

You can also model the use of a role play area for the children, with the help of another practitioner. For instance showing how the 'booking in' area at the Garage could work, by modelling the conversation that a customer has when she brings in her car for repair. Use the list of environments and mark making/language activities below to inspire you:

- ✓ **Shoe shop** – boxes, shoes, shoe size chart and measuring ruler, order forms, receipts, tills.
- ✓ **Post office** – scales, phone, different sized envelopes, stampers, stationery, parcel wrapping with brown paper and tape, labels.
- ✓ **Garage** – tickets for car wash, office and reception area, booking in form, diary, calendar, car repair handbooks, telephones, role play vehicles, outdoor chalk for marking out 'bays', tools.
- ✓ **Restaurant** – cooking, weighing, writing recipes, ingredients, shopping, menus, order pads.
- ✓ **Airport** – x-ray machine to 'scan' cases, airline tickets, boarding passes, security area, lines of chairs to make the 'plane', suitcases, scales, labels, passports.

    ✓ **Garden centre** – plants, price tags, tools, tills, café area, catalogues, seed packets, planting demonstration.
    ✓ **Clothes shop** – clothes rail, mirror, price tags, hangers, changing rooms, tills, dressing up clothes, hats, bags, belts, shoes.
    ✓ **Hairdressers** – mirrors, scissors, 'Girl's World' head, diary, pictures of different hair styles, magazines, till, telephones.

If you have space, in a nursery/preschool it is useful to have a 'home corner' on offer all the time with the usual kitchen items, sink, cooker, etc. Your role play area can, if space allows, be in addition to this. Don't forget that a role play area can also be located outside, for instance a 'beach' area in the summer months.

Deconstructed role play

The idea of 'deconstructed role play' is that you offer the children a variety of multipurpose materials with which they can role play as they wish. Rather than directing their play through the kind of role play area you set up, the children get to use their imaginations. Your materials might include:

    ✓ Lots of large pieces of material;
    ✓ Tarpaulins;
    ✓ Pegs;
    ✓ String and rope;
    ✓ Cardboard boxes in all different sizes;
    ✓ Sheets of flat cardboard/Perspex;
    ✓ Pipes, bricks;
    ✓ Cardboard tubes and rolls;
    ✓ Sellotape, masking tape, parcel tape.

Themes for writing

Themes and topics have gone a little bit out of favour in the early years in recent times. If we truly plan to follow the children's interests, and let them initiate most of the learning, then clearly a theme is a bit of an adult imposition. However, I'm a great believer in themes, for a number of very good reasons:

    ✓ They bring the writing/learning to life, and give it a clear purpose;

✓ They are often inspired by, or lead on to, a trip somewhere out-side of the school or nursery;
✓ They offer the children access to ideas, information and experi-ences that they might not otherwise have;
✓ They show how learning is linked – how the study of a theme links to skills and ideas in all different areas of the curriculum;
✓ They just feel 'right' to me, instinctively, as a way of inspiring my teaching, and the children's learning.

At nursery/preschool age, you can use 'mini' themes which inform your planning in some areas of learning. The children can still initiate their own learning, but you offer them access to fresh ideas and new experiences in some of your continuous provision. Here are a few ideas for inspirational themes, along with suggestions about how they might lead to language learning and mark making across the curriculum:

✓ **Outer Space** – building a rocket (we used a giant cardboard box – wardrobe size from a well known storage company), silver foil, astronaut training school, count down to take off, map of space, labels of the different planets, model of the solar system, star maps, going outside on a dark winter afternoon to look at the stars/moon, art using silver pens on a black background.
✓ **Fireworks Night** – safety posters, scratch art of fireworks (col-our the paper with stripes of different coloured crayons, then paint over with black paint and scratch out your fireworks), poems about firework noises, using percussion instruments to make a 'fireworks soundtrack'.
✓ **Under the Sea** – a visit to an aquarium, making fact cards about different sea creatures, giant 'under the water' collage scene with labels, books such as Julia Donaldson's '*Sharing a Shell*', stories from films such as *Finding Nemo*.
✓ **The Great Fire of London** – a trip to London to see the sights, 'fire' pictures using black silhouettes and red/yellow tissue paper flames, 3D pictures made inside a cardboard box, writing a diary entry about how the fire started, making a brainstorm together of words connected to fire.

As well as choosing a theme yourself to bring fresh learning to the chil-dren, you can also develop a theme based on the children's current inter-ests. For instance the 'superhero' theme described below (in 'Inspiring your boys').

Mark making in the outdoors

The outdoors offers a fantastic environment for mark making. Where possible, it is great if you can give young children the chance to 'free flow' between indoors and outdoors, at least for part of the day. The many positives of outdoor play, and mark making in the outdoors, include:

- ✓ There is much less pressure to keep tidy and clean;
- ✓ It's much easier to clean up (washing paint off the ground with a hose);
- ✓ The outdoors lends itself well to mucky and multisensory play;
- ✓ It's a multisensory environment in and of itself – the wind, the sun, the bird song (or the traffic noise);
- ✓ It encourages independence, for instance children putting on their coats by themselves before they come outside;
- ✓ The children can make choices about their play, and experiment with different natural materials (mud, sand, water, leaves, stones);
- ✓ For older children, it offers a break from the routine of the classroom, and a chance to let off steam.

In a free flow nursery or preschool setting, your boys will often choose to play outdoors rather than indoors. This means that it is essential to offer plenty of chances to make marks in the outdoor area. You might be:

- ✓ Practising writing letter shapes or numbers on the playground floor in chalk;
- ✓ Making a 'welcome mat' just outside the door to your inside area;
- ✓ Brainstorming words around a theme, each theme contained in a circle (draw around the inside of a hula hoop);
- ✓ Marking 'bays' for the ride on toys, and labelling the ride on toys with a number. Number the bays and the toys and get the children to park them in the right place;
- ✓ Painting on long strips of lining paper (either pegged up on a wall or laid flat on the ground);
- ✓ Going on a sensory walk and recording what you see through photographs, drawings and recordings.

In the photograph below you can see Shay having great fun in our outdoor area. The mark making activity began with the suggestion that the children might want to paint using the long grasses that you see in the photograph. Shay and some of the other children decided to paint their hands and make hand prints as well.

The practicalities

If you're working in a nursery, preschool or nursery class you are likely to be spending a lot of time outdoors with your children, particularly if they are able to free flow between indoors and outdoors as they wish. There are various practicalities to consider, for instance you may need to buy:

✓ High quality waterproof suits, as you can see in the photograph above, which keep the children warm and dry whatever the weather;

✓ Bright 'high vis' jackets for the children and adults to wear when you go out on a walk or a trip;

✓ A cover for shade in the summer and to keep dry in the winter – if you have the funding, invest in a permanent covered area. We use a professional quality marquee because ours is a pack away setting;

✓ A 'free flow' curtain, made of PVC strips, to keep the heat indoors when the door is open;

✓ A storage rack for wellies.

If you possibly can, get some plants growing in your outdoor area, and incorporate an area for wildlife as well. You might look at your space and think that this wouldn't be possible, but it's surprising what you can achieve in a small area. At our preschool, we were given a tiny strip of disused land alongside our hall to make a garden. The ground was tarmac, so we had to use raised beds (you could use pots for a similar effect). We got parents and local businesses involved, and it really didn't cost us a huge amount of money to create our garden. You can see part of the result in the photo below. The children gain a huge amount of sensory, fine motor and other writing related experiences from being able to dig in the earth and watch plants grow.

It's a great idea to create a portable 'grab and go' writing toolkit for your-self, based on the kind of writing activities your children like to do out-doors. Your kit could include items such as mini clipboards, a pair of scissors, glue, sticky tape, pens and pencils, paper, envelopes, outdoor chalks, tape measures and compasses.

∗   ∗   ∗

Practical project – Making a map

You will need

- ✓ A map of your local area;
- ✓ A set of clipboards with paper and pencils;
- ✓ For older children, compasses.

Learning intentions

- ✓ Showing that mark making has a purpose – that it can help you record locations;
- ✓ Showing how a map can help you and others find your way around.

Instructions

Take your children out to explore their local environment, so that they can make a mental and literal 'map' of the different locations. Help them to identify the key locations that they wish to record – the sweet shop, a local park, a friend's house that you pass and so on.

During your walk, use the language of directions to encourage spatial awareness and a widening vocabulary. Use words such as up, down, around, next to or over. When you've finished your map, get others to follow it to see if they can read it correctly.

∗   ∗   ∗

Inspiring your boys

When talking about how to inspire boys, it is necessary to engage in some generalizations. These are often things that teachers and practitioners feel instinctively about how boys and girls play and learn. While these are generalized comments which won't apply to every child, on the whole, boys tend to:

- ✓ Enjoy getting messy and dirty;
- ✓ Like games that involve physical activity;

✓ Like using language in a 'rude' way, for example toilet humour;
✓ Love exploring how things go together, and how they are taken apart;
✓ Like to know how things work, and to experiment with them;
✓ Prefer non-fiction to stories;
✓ Prefer stories that are about action and adventure;
✓ Like to watch and read cartoons;
✓ Like factual and reference books;
✓ Are good at following step by step instructions;
✓ Come to both reading and writing later than girls;
✓ Find it harder to handle writing tools than girls do;
✓ Are less interested in being neat and writing correctly;
✓ Are less interested in colouring in and decorating activities;
✓ Are more interested in playing outside;
✓ Tend to be at their most inspired when they really 'get into' a specific character, book series or TV show (for instance the *Beast Quest* books by Adam Blade are very popular at the moment);
✓ Enjoy an element of challenge and competition.

In the picture, you can see a very detailed child-initiated piece of writing/drawing done by a 6-year-old boy. The child was very much into the cartoon character 'Spongebob', and was also very keen on cartoons and comics. As you can see in the picture, he has taken the original character and turned it into the 'Spongetron at Work'. He is using elements of the cartoon genre such as speech bubbles and graphic writing.

The generalizations above can lead you to some useful techniques for inspiring boys in their mark making. For instance to inspire your boys, make sure that you:

- ✓ Offer a range of texts, including plenty of non-fiction and forms such as comics, instruction booklets and packaging materials;
- ✓ Have lots of different mark making materials on offer outside, including plenty of mucky options such as writing with or in mud;
- ✓ Set up role plays to inspire your boys, such as astronauts going into space or superhero squads;
- ✓ Get your class to write in a range of forms – instruction booklets as well as stories, top trump dinosaur cards as well as fairy tale character cards;
- ✓ Base activities around cartoon characters and other 'boy friendly' characters, as well as the more traditional fairy tale figures.

* * *

Practical project: Superhero squad

You will need

- ✓ Superhero comics;
- ✓ A den or climbing frame;
- ✓ Superhero costumes;
- ✓ Silver foil, paper and craft materials (as required);
- ✓ Various mark making tools.

Learning intentions

- ✓ To inspire your boys to want to make marks.

Instructions

This project followed a period of huge interest from our boys in being superheroes. Many of them were turning up to preschool each day dressed in their superhero costumes. Clearly, a 'Super-hero Base' was required!

We set up a large wooden climbing frame, and wrapped it in paper and offered materials with which the children could decorate it. This was then used by the children (both boys and girls) to create their Super-hero Den – a place where the superheroes could come to meet up and share their stories. (Later on, the Den became a Princess Palace, for knights and princesses.)

By offering plenty of superhero comics alongside this role play, the boys were encouraged to see how writing and mark making related to their favourite story characters.

* * *

From Letters to Words, from Words to Sentences 8

In this section . . .

- Help your children move from mark making to forming letters
- Help your children move from forming letters to writing words
- Build confidence in the early stages of writing
- Understand how spelling accuracy develops
- Support your children in developing good handwriting

Consider this . . .

The final phase of learning to write involves teaching your children how to sound out and form letters, and how to blend and segment words. This part of the process requires persistence, determination and lots and lots of repetition. It is not something that children will pick up through osmosis – it must be taught through adult-directed, adult-initiated and adult-supervised activities, rather than being picked up via child-initiated learning. It can of course still be done more freely during child-initiated time – the children using their new found knowledge to take orders in your role play café, and so on. At this early stage reinforcement is key, whether this means reinforcing the letter sound, the correct way to form the letter shape or how to blend or segment the words. Bad habits picked up at this age (poor pencil grip, incorrect letter formation) can stay with a child for life – this is a hugely important phase of a child's education.

Reading and writing are very much equal partners in the process of becoming literate (with talking and listening playing a vital role as well). Reading is incredibly important in feeding into writing, and in helping the child develop a wide and fluent vocabulary in his written work. Phonics is crucial in the early stages of reading and writing, especially for the less able children. However, eventually your young writers will need to move beyond the need to sound out every word in order to spell it. If I see a word a hundred, a thousand, even a million times on a page when I'm reading, then I start to get comfy with the shape, the look, even the feel of it spelt correctly. The current emphasis on synthetic phonics makes this sound a bit like heresy, but how would I ever learn to spell and write tough, bough, cough and dough purely through phonic knowledge? Even as an adult, when I'm writing and I come across a word that I can't remember how to spell, I rely as much on my knowledge of whether the word *looks* right as to how it might be sounded out.

Interestingly, the same link between wide and avid reading applies to the acquisition of grammatical knowledge, and also to children finding their own writing 'voice'. Yes, you can teach your children the 'naming of parts' – what a subordinate clause looks like, how to spot and use a noun, a verb, an adjective or a connective. But if I read plenty of grammatically correct writing (and indeed hear grammatically correct English being spoken), I learn to speak it for myself in my own writing. Equally, if I hear the voices of thousands of different writers, I start to develop a feel for what 'works', and what kind of writing 'voice' I would like for myself.

From marks to letters – learning to read

There are approximately 44 phonemes in the English language (the exact number depends on the accent of the speaker). When you introduce the initial letter sounds to your children, model the *actual sound* for them rather than adding an 'uh' to the letter to make what we might describe as a 'letter sound'. So, the letter 's' is pronounced as 'sss' rather than as 'suh'. This will help them a great deal when it comes to blending the sounds together to make words ('sss – a – ttt' rather than 'suh – ah – tuh').

The structure of the learning

As children move into the first year of statutory schooling, more time is spent on adult-directed literacy teaching than in the nursery or preschool years. In a typical Reception class there will be a focus on literacy and/or phonics each day, for between 20 and 40 minutes. There will also be focused small group activities supported by a teacher or teaching assistant and plenty of child-initiated learning, perhaps around a topic or a theme. As the children move into Key Stage One, this time will lengthen to about an hour (often called the 'Literacy Hour' in English schools).

It's worth remember that children of this age still have a short concentration span – typically, after 10 or 15 minutes they will benefit from a break or a change in the type of task. When you begin to introduce letters to your class, there are a number of important teaching techniques to use to ensure the most effective approach:

✓ Use a fast pace, so that the children stay engaged and focused in your literacy time;

✓ Move quickly through the learning, so that the children can almost immediately begin to form some words of their own;

✓ Incorporate lots of repetition – find opportunities throughout the day/week to practise the sounds and to form the letters;

✓ Revise and refer back to what has gone before, incorporating it into child-initiated learning, as well as into adult-directed teaching;

✓ Keep the learning interactive, physical, practical, kinaesthetic – make it really hands-on to 'stick' it in your children's minds;

✓ Use mnemonics and other memory tricks to help your children remember;

✓ Encourage your children to think about ways of remembering sounds and spellings, really picking apart and working with the language right from the start;

✓ Get support from parents – encourage them to revisit the learning at home so that you can move on quickly;

✓ Ensure that you maintain the children's confidence, especially for the weaker children;

✓ Keep an eye out for the strugglers, identifying and getting support in place for them early on;

✓ Watch out too for any children who are absent early on – support these children in learning the sounds that they have missed;

✓ Keep an eye out for the more able children as well, and ensure that they are challenged and stretched, especially if they are already able to read.

You'll often have a very wide spread of ability and previous experience in this age group. Some children may not have attended a preschool or nursery and the Reception class will be the first time they have been in a large group setting with their peers. Consequently, they may struggle with social skills and with more structured aspects of the day such as sitting on the carpet. Similarly, you may also have children who have learnt to read at home, and who are ready to get going straight away on their writing.

Learning letter/sound correspondences

The procedure for learning a new letter/sound correspondence (or grapheme/phoneme correspondence) follows a similar pattern each time: the revisit/review, teach, practise, apply pattern, as described in the Letters and Sounds materials (see the companion website for the relevant internet links). Of course, the teacher can make the various parts of the process as interesting, interactive, multisensory and resource-based as he or she is able! The usual pattern is to:

- ✓ Introduce the letter to the group or class;
- ✓ Say the sound;
- ✓ Get the children to say the sound;
- ✓ Reinforce the learning through kinaesthetic, visual or other means (e.g. show the children the action that matches the sound as in the 'Jolly Phonics' programme);
- ✓ Put the sound into context, that is identifying or demonstrating toys, objects, people, places, etc. with that sound in them;
- ✓ Play games or complete activities to reinforce the learning of the sound.

Structured phonics programmes

The vast majority of schools in the United Kingdom now use some kind of systematic synthetic phonics programme to teach literacy (Jolly Phonics, Letterland, Read Write Inc, Letters and Sounds, etc.). Clearly, using a systematic programme has a large number of benefits:

- ✓ It saves time and effort for the teacher when it comes to planning literacy lessons;

✓ Often, the relevant resources are included (flash cards, work sheets, posters), again saving time for the teacher;

✓ The structured nature of the programme means that all the phonemes are covered, in a logical order;

✓ The teacher feels confident that he is offering the children a tried and tested method for learning to read;

✓ The less able children, or those with learning difficulties, benefit from a highly structured approach.

However, there are downsides to using a very structured programme – these programmes can, by their very nature, be rather repetitive and creatively limited (particularly in the writing strand). They may also tempt you to hold back an able child who just wants to get on with her reading. Certainly, when I first trained as an early years teacher, there were very few of these structured programmes on offer. Amazingly we still managed to teach the children how to read through using a mix of approaches that worked for each individual, including, but not limited to, synthetic phonics. Where you use a clearly structured programme, take care that:

✗ You don't feel that you must follow the programme slavishly, using all the materials, ideas and approaches provided, instead of considering what would work best for your children;

✗ You give a context to the learning, remembering that words have a *meaning* as well as a set of sounds, and that reading is about meaning, not simply about decoding what the words say;

✗ You don't rule out other approaches, or make the children feel bad about using their own techniques (for instance using context to figure out what a word might say);

✗ You give plenty of support to the children in learning to read and spell words which are not spelt in a regular way (often called 'tricky words');

✗ You introduce the children to a variety of ways of learning spellings, including those to do with whole word recognition and looking at the shapes of words;

✗ You maintain the *joy* of reading for your children, by sharing and working with plenty of stories and other texts;

✗ You offer plenty of chances for free writing, where getting meaning across is the aim, and not just writing tasks that involve repeated practice of a new sound.

Letter (and word) hunts

Children adore the idea of hunting for 'treasure'; capitalize on this interest by taking them on a letter or a word hunt. The children might:

✓ Hunt for letters hidden outside in a garden or in the school grounds, and use them to create words;

✓ Use a magnifying glass to find miniature words or letters hidden within your classroom;

✓ Find 'secret letters/words' written in invisible ink, as though they are spies;

✓ Hunt for letters and words in different forms and formats – on cereal packets, on displays around the school, in story books or in comics;

✓ 'Bury' a word that they don't like – I once heard a story about a teacher who got her class to do a funeral for the word 'nice' because she hated them using it so much.

* * *

 ## Practical project: 'Letter of the Day' or 'Letters of the Week' area

You will need

✓ A set of letters (or single letter) on which you'd like to focus;

✓ Lots of objects starting with those letters, or objects that have those sounds in them;

✓ Plastic or magnetic letters and a magnetic board;

✓ Laminated letter cards showing the correct formation;

✓ Large examples of the letters, for display on your walls.

Learning intentions

✓ To reinforce the children's learning of specific letters and sounds;

✓ To match sounds with letters;

✓ To make handwriting practice more engaging;

✓ To link home and school to support literacy learning.

Instructions

Create a 'Letter of the Day/Week' area within your classroom to help the children reinforce what they have learned in their phonics/literacy time. Incorporate plenty of resources and free choice activities within this area to reinforce the learning that has taken place in adult-directed sessions. For instance you could:

✓ Have a table with lots of resources on it that start with this letter or letters;
✓ Set the children the challenge of sorting the objects according to the letter they start with;
✓ Ask the children to bring in something from home which starts with that letter;
✓ Have interactive games available on a laptop, for the children to play within the area;
✓ Create a 'treasure hunt' where the children have to find examples of these letters hidden around your classroom, in an area outdoors, in the sand, in a feely bag by touch alone and so on;
✓ Put a box of Lego and a Lego board in the area so that children can form letters and words out of the bricks.

*   *   *

From marks to letters – learning to write

Although reading and writing typically develop alongside each other during the first couple of years of school, writing is much harder for most children than reading. In order to be able to write, they have to:

✓ Work out what they want to say or talk about in their writing;
✓ Have the confidence to commit those ideas or thoughts to paper;
✓ Work out how to spell the words that they want to write down;
✓ Form the words on the page in a legible way.

A key aspect of this phase of the journey is the way that the teacher maintains each child's confidence and motivation to write.

Learning letter formation

When introducing the formation of individual letters, a similar pattern is usually taken to that which we use for teaching how to sound out letters and phonemes:

✓ Model how the letter is written for the whole class;
✓ Get the children to use a kinaesthetic approach to write the letter (trace it on your hand, trace it on the back of the child in front of you, write it in the air);
✓ Write the letter as a whole group using a writing tool (on a mini whiteboard with a marker pen, on the interactive whiteboard);
✓ Write the letter individually, using pencil on paper, reinforcing the learning through regular practice.

Teachers will often introduce the letter sound and the letter formation – the reading and the writing – simultaneously. This would seem to make sense – why tell a child how to read a letter and then not let her write it? Some educators argue, however, that children are ready to read much earlier than they are physically ready to write. My preferred approach is to introduce both aspects simultaneously.

Teaching letter formation

Here are some useful ideas for teaching your children to form their letters correctly, and encouraging them to practice the skills required while remaining engaged and interested. As well as using these techniques, use the checklists of 'Make marks with' and 'Make marks on' that you can find in the Appendix of this book, to inspire how you resource your classroom.

✓ Offer 'trace over' cards, with a green arrow for the start point, and a red stop sign for the end point.
✓ Show how letters are formed on your interactive whiteboard (have an animation running over and over, depending on the letter or letters you are studying).
✓ Write the children's names on your interactive whiteboard, and get the children to trace over them. Gradually make them smaller, and when they are confident add their surnames.
✓ Create laminated name cards for the children to use first thing in the morning, to self-register. Ask them to trace over their name as accurately as possible, then post it in your class postbox.
✓ Offer laminated letter mats, strips or cards which show the correct formation (and the joins in cursive writing). Supervise

the use of these to ensure that the children learn correct letter
formation.

✓ Get the children to be the teacher and correct your letter formation – write a letter in the 'wrong way' on the board – what did
you do wrong and how can they correct you?

✓ Try this lovely 'rainbow letters' activity – offer the children a set
of pencils matching the colours of the rainbow. They must trace
over a letter with each colour of the rainbow in turn – by the
time they do violet, the letter should have turned black!

You can find a link to a free set of downloadable letter formation cards
in the companion website.

From letters to words

As soon as the children have the first few sets of letters under their belts,
they can start to blend and segment simple regular Consonant Vowel
Consonant (CVC) words such as 'cat', 'dog' and 'tin'. To help support
this process try splitting up words as you talk, during the course of
your daily routine: 'Who knows where I've put my p – e – n?' or 'I want
B – e – n to answer the next question.'

Get your children building 'banks' of letters, phonemes and words to
use in their writing, in lots of different ways. For instance you could:

✓ Have a 'bank' of graphemes on your classroom wall, listed
according to their connected sounds, which you regularly work
through with the class. (Many of the structured reading programmes include a list of these for you to display.)

✓ Build a 'bank' of words together on a topic, to put in a topic display
area. Write the words on laminated cards which you attach to the
wall with Velcro. The children can then use these in their writing.

✓ Brainstorm key vocabulary for a writing activity together on your
interactive whiteboard, to act as a 'bank' while they write.

✓ Have a bank of 'tricky words' available on the wall for the children
to take and use whenever they wish to write them – regularly
used tricky words such as 'the', 'said', 'no', 'go', 'some', etc.

✓ Keep a small 'word book' in which children record the words
they use under the letters of the alphabet.

✓ Get your children to write out any words they find hard to spell
three times in a 'bank' at the back of a writing book.

✓ Create long lists of words, all using the same phoneme, or phonemes that follow the same pattern. This works well as a home-
work task, where the parents can support and assist their child.
For instance a list of words for: ar, er and ir; or ch, sh and th; or
u-e, oo and ew.
✓ Buy magnetic sets of words for your class to use whenever they
need.

It's also very useful to give your children access to the most commonly
used words, both those that can be spelt phonetically, and those that they
must learn in other ways. You can find links to useful internet sources
for 'commonly used words' in the companion website.

Learning tricky words

As you'll be aware, English is not a regular language. Over the centu-
ries, it has 'borrowed' many words from other languages and has been
influenced by many other cultures. It has also evolved as a language, for
instance where people started to pronounce a word differently, while still
spelling it the same. Some of the key irregularities in English include:

✓ Words with a silent letter – such as know and gnat.
✓ Words with the same letter combination – such as 'ough' – but
with a multitude of different pronunciations. Consider how you
would say the following: thought, enough, through, though,
bough.
✓ There are many words that are spelt differently, but which sound
the same, such as 'their' and 'there' (homophones).
✓ Confusingly, there are also homonyms – words which are spelt
the same, but pronounced differently, such as 'wind' (up a clock)
and 'wind' (as in the weather).

A key part of helping your children learn how to write is giving them
strategies for those situations where a word cannot easily be decoded
or spelt using phonic knowledge. This is why reading is so vital – they
can internalize the spelling of the irregular words which they see over
and over again. Teach them how to remember the spelling of a word in
a range of different ways:

✓ **By sight and shape** – encourage them to examine the shape of the word – which bits are high, which bits are low, does it have a flat or a bumpy shape? What does the overall shape look like? For instance the word 'the' has a very particular visual shape (at least to my mind).

✓ **By repetition** – getting the tricky word into the child's visual or physical memory by seeing or writing the word shape over and over again.

✓ **By focusing and thinking** – examining which bit of the word does not fit the regular pattern and working out a way to remember it. For instance the word 'want' is pronounced 'wont', so tell your children to say it as 'want' with an emphasis on the 'a'.

✓ **By using a mnemonic** – the classic is 'big elephants can always understand small elephants' for spelling the word 'because'. Mnemonics are also great for helping children remember how to spell regular combinations such as 'ould' – as in, 'oh you little darling'.

✓ **By making connections** – many children find the spelling of the word 'said' tricky to remember, and will write it as 'siad' instead. If you talk about how the word 'said' is formed from the word 'say' it all starts to make sense.

✓ **By exploring the roots** – 'one', 'once' and 'only' clearly come from the same root, meaning a single unit of something.

✓ **By exploring the country or language of origin** – the word 'beautiful' has 'beau' from the French in it; the combination 'psych' comes from 'mind'.

✓ **By adding a fun and physical element** – when you're teaching lists of homophones, get the children to 'kick the letter out of the way'. For instance to make 'sun' become 'son' they must 'kick the u out of the way'. Get them to stand up and practice doing it.

Teaching cursive handwriting

Depending on the policy at your school, you might start your children out with print, then move onto cursive (or joined up) handwriting at about age 6 or 7. Alternatively, you might be expected to start with cursive from the beginning. Often, it's a matter of habit, in that the teacher or school has always taught writing in a particular way. It's even a matter of nationality, with different countries taking different approaches. It's worth considering the various points for and against teaching cursive from the start, rather than print. On the plus side with cursive:

- ✔ The children don't have to learn a whole new writing style when they come to join up their letters;
- ✔ Cursive flows more easily across the page;
- ✔ Cursive writing can help the children develop a physical memory of how letters are formed;
- ✔ Because the letters flow from the left to the right, this tends to help children not to mix up letters such as b and d;
- ✔ It is recommended by the British Dyslexia Association that children who have dyslexia write in a cursive style from the start.

On the minus side with cursive:

- ✕ Most story books are written in print, so it is easier for the children to read and write in this style;
- ✕ Most early years resources and posters use print, rather than cursive;
- ✕ Printing is easier for small hands, and the letters can be easily separated out;
- ✕ Cursive handwriting takes quite a bit of confidence, and less able children might find it hard to form words at first;
- ✕ Cursive handwriting can look messy in early stages, as the movements are harder than those needed to print letters.

Overall, it's very much a matter of personal preference and habit. Some of the issues above can be overcome by teaching children their original print letters with 'entry strokes' and 'exit strokes', so that they are ready to move onto joining up their letters easily.

When teaching handwriting, give your children plenty of time to practise, for instance having a regular slot during morning drop off and registration time. Younger children could practise their letter formation at this time, for about 5 minutes each day. Older children (able Year 1 children and Year 2 children) could be given 10 minutes practice each day at entry/exit strokes and cursive writing.

There is no one 'correct' order in which to teach the cursive strokes, although the movement required to join 'c' to 'c' is commonly taught first. You can find some useful links about cursive handwriting in the companion website.

Teaching punctuation

At this stage, punctuation takes its very simplest forms. As you introduce each punctuation mark to your class, make sure that you help the children understand *what the punctuation mark does* as well as where it goes. What that means is, talk about the logic and purpose of a full stop or a capital letter within a piece of writing, as well as just telling them that it goes at the beginning or end of a sentence. Talk about the idea of one sentence containing a single set of ideas, and similarly about how commas can be used to separate a sequence of details within a sentence, or to indicate a pause.

As with the teaching of reading and writing, ensure that you teach punctuation in a physical and kinaesthetic way. Get your children reading a sentence – stretching up to make the big capital letter at the start, and then 'punching out' a full stop to end it. Encourage them to take a breath before they begin to read the next sentence – you could describe this as 'sucking in some more super reading energy'. With commas, use a little 'hiccough' between each one to show how it feels to read a series of items on a list, as opposed to a longer pause between sentences after a full stop. Again, much of their knowledge about punctuation will develop as they become wide and avid readers. For many more ideas on teaching punctuation to your writers, see my book for teachers working with older children, *Getting the Buggers to Write* (Third edition) (Continuum, 2011).

Building writing confidence

There is often a lot of pressure on teachers to push their children on with their reading and writing. This pressure comes from all different directions – from parents, from local authority inspectors, from the Department of Education and often from the head teacher as well. However, children of course develop this skill at very different rates. Because literacy learning is often done in a whole class session, some children may struggle to keep up and to retain what has previously been learned. Where children start to lag behind, this can damage their confidence and put them off the very thing that you want them to feel happy about doing – writing! Make sure that you:

- ✓ Strike a balance between correcting bad habits (especially with letter formation) and correcting so much and so often that the child feels constantly under pressure to 'get it right'.
- ✓ Use copying activities, particularly for those children who lack confidence. Write a word or sentence for the child to copy below (or have it available in print for them to copy).
- ✓ Use lots of 'fill in the blanks' type activities, where some or most of the sentence has already been written for the child (the structured programmes often come with 'work books' where the child practises using this technique).
- ✓ Use tracing activities, to reinforce correct handwriting technique.
- ✓ Make sure you don't forget to give plenty of time and opportunities for 'free writing' where the children can simply write what they want, without any pressure to spell correctly or to write neatly.
- ✓ Allow the children plenty of chances to use ICT, so that they can write via typing as well as via handwriting.
- ✓ Write as a whole class, with the children giving you their ideas and you scribing them on the board.
- ✓ 'Write' via non written methods, for instance letting the children audio/video record their ideas, stories, etc.
- ✓ Offer the children 'sentence starters' on laminated strips, to use in their writing.
- ✓ Teach techniques for getting ideas – brainstorming and mind mapping, the use of 'who, what, why, when, where and how'.
- ✓ Offer the children writing frames and structures – the layout of a recipe form, the outline of a 'thank you' card.

With your young writers, build confidence by finding opportunities for them to write individual words. For instance:

- ✓ Adding labels to a class display;
- ✓ Writing their name on a piece of work;
- ✓ Filling in the blanks ('cloze procedure') activities;
- ✓ Copying the same sentence over and over, with one word replaced each time ('I can spin', 'I can hop', 'I can jump');
- ✓ Creating 'character cards' (i.e. character studies) from the books you read, listing single words that refer to the character.

Copying writing

Some teachers dislike the idea of using 'copying' activities because they feel that they limit the expressive purpose for which language is being used. However, where children need to build confidence in their writing or where they have a particular interest but not the vocabulary required to express it, copying activities can be very useful. In a way, copying from real life examples of writing is just as valid as copying from what the teacher has modelled on the board.

In the example above, the 6-year-old child has done an incredibly detailed piece of writing based on the Lego 'Power Miners' characters. This writing was self-initiated, with the child copying information from magazines and Lego boxes and instructions to create a very convincing piece of writing.

Connecting writing

The final stage in this age group is when the children begin to create longer sentences, by starting to use connectives. You can find a useful list of connectives for your young writers in the companion website. Again, talk to the children about the logic behind using connecting words – that they can join up two short sentences to make a longer one. They can also show how events link together, how one event might cause another or the sequence in which events come.

It can be tricky for children of this age to use connectives in a fluent way, to make these longer sentences, while still maintaining meaning within their writing. Often they will use them to show a sequence of events, but within short sentences. You can see this in the piece of writing below, where the details of the trip to Westonbirt are clearly given in sequence, but the sentences are still short and choppy.

This example of writing was done as an adult-directed activity by a 5-year-old child in Year 1.

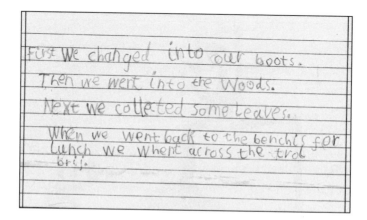

Dyslexia

You will come across some children who really struggle to pick up the basics of reading and writing. You will need to decide whether they are just not ready yet, or whether they have a more serious learning difficulty such as Dyslexia. Dyslexia is a learning difficulty which mainly affects a person's ability to read, write and spell. A child who has dyslexia will display a variety of symptoms, including the following:

- ✓ He seems generally bright and able in some areas, but struggles particularly with reading, writing and spelling;
- ✓ She has difficulty sustaining attention, and may appear to 'zone out';
- ✓ He has poor coordination and his motor skills are generally slow to develop;

- ✓ Some of her attempts at spelling are bizarre, and do not seem to follow phonic patterns that the class has learnt;
- ✓ His pencil grip is weak or poor, and he finds it hard to stay close to the margin when starting a piece of writing;
- ✓ She persistently confuses similar looking letters – b/d, p/g, m/w;
- ✓ There are lots of crossings out in his work, and lots of attempts to spell a word in different ways;
- ✓ She finds it hard to keep time properly, and has poor personal organization skills;
- ✓ He has difficulty remembering sequences – days of the week, the alphabet.

For useful internet links on the symptoms, identification and treatment of dyslexia, visit the companion website.

If you suspect that a child has dyslexia, make sure that you refer him for a specialist assessment. In the meantime, all the various approaches described in this book will be of benefit to the child.

And finally, I'd like to wish you and your children all the best of luck on your journey along the road to writing. It's a long road, with plenty of challenges along the way, but the destination is a truly wonderful place.

Checklists and Audits

The checklists and audit forms that follow are designed to get you reflecting on your setting, and the way it is resourced and laid out. These forms should help you get all the appropriate equipment and tools in place, for your children's journey down the road to writing. They also act as a reminder of all those great ideas that float around within schools, books and across the internet.

 Visit the companion website for downloadable versions of all the checklists and audit forms.

'Make marks with' checklist

Do you offer your children access to all of these resources for mark making in your setting?

We make marks with . . .	Tick
Chalk	☐
Felt pens	☐
Pencils	☐
Biros	☐
Large marker pens	☐
Dry wipe marker pens	☐
Charcoal	☐
Oil pastels	☐
Water colour pastels	☐
Paint brushes	☐
Tooth brushes	☐
Sponges	☐
Stampers	☐
String and wool	☐
Twigs, grasses and other natural materials	☐
Silver, gold and other metallic pens	☐

We make marks with . . .	Tick
'Magic' water (water with glitter in it)	☐
Marbles	☐
Toys – cars, animals	☐
Our bodies – fingers, hands, toes, feet	☐
Food – fruit and vegetable prints	☐
Food – finger painting with chocolate	☐
Highlighter pens	☐
Stones (for making patterns)	☐
Coloured sands in shaker containers	☐
Glitter shakers	☐
Play dough and clay letter sculptures	☐
Shaving brushes	☐
Watered down paint in water squirters	☐
Hole punchers	☐

'Make marks on' checklist

Do you offer your children the chance to make marks on all different kinds of surfaces?

Resource	Tick
Diaries	☐
Calendars	☐
Post it notes	☐
Birthday cards	☐
Mini individual whiteboards	☐
Large whiteboards	☐
An interactive whiteboard	☐
Full size clipboards	☐
Mini clipboards with pencils attached	☐
A1 size flipchart paper	☐
White paper	☐
Coloured paper	☐
Lined paper	☐

Resource	Tick
Squared paper	☐
Scrolls of paper	☐
Cardboard boxes	☐
Large flat sheets of cardboard	☐
Mini chalkboards	☐
Large chalkboard	☐
Outdoor walls	☐
Sheets of old/recycled wood or Medium-density fibreboard (MDF)	☐
Envelopes	☐
Postcards	☐
Long rolls of lining paper	☐
Rolls of wallpaper – with different textured surfaces	☐
Clay	☐
Play dough	☐
Mirrors	☐
Stencils	☐
Paper taped *under* a table, as in a den	☐
Paper taped *onto* a table	☐
Sheets of foil (scratch with an old pen or stick)	☐
Etch a sketch	☐
The ground outside	☐
The entrance to your setting (a 'doormat' in chalk)	☐
Shed walls	☐
A 'Graffiti wall' (see p. 90 for details)	☐
Second hand or old and unused furniture, for example decorating chairs	☐
Fences	☐
Sand	☐
Mud	☐
Laminated name cards for tracing over	☐

'Space as a resource' checklist

Does your space fulfil all the following criteria?

Resource	Tick
A dedicated 'Writing Area' for free choice or focused writing	☐
A dedicated 'Reading Area' with soft seating	☐
A dedicated 'Listening Area' where it is quiet so the children can focus	☐
Easily accessible resources that the children can use as/when they wish	☐
A mixture of resources, regularly checked and audited for relevance	☐
Interesting displays, at a level where the children can see them	☐
Feels open, uncluttered, easy for teacher/children to move around	☐
Different areas divided off or partitioned in some way from each other	☐
Welcoming to parents and children	☐
Displays in a variety of community languages, as appropriate	☐
Visual displays, signs and symbols	☐
Layout allows for differentiated small group activities	☐
Comfy places for children to go to relax	☐
Displays to inform staff, as well as for the children	☐
Access to ICT for a variety of different activities	☐

'Space and communication' audit

Where does most of the talking happen within our space?

Is most of the talking adult to child, child to child or adult to adult?

Where does most of the listening happen within our space?

Who does most listening – children or adults?

Are there any 'hot spots' where behaviour is a particular issue?

How many 'high impact' activities are there? (These might be ones that require close adult supervision, or ones that are particularly noisy or excitable.)

How do the children move around the space? Do they follow the 'golden rules' even when adults are not watching?

'Displays' audit

What do you first notice about the space?

What displays do you notice first?

What colours were first to catch your eye?

What colour or colours seem to predominate within the space?

Are you seeing mainly: children's work, adult's work or pre-printed materials?

Are the displays at a child's height or an adult's height?

Does the space feel cluttered or empty or just right?

If you could use one word to describe the displays, what would it be?